YOG
AND T
BHAGAVAD-GITA

YOGA AND THE BHAGAVAD-GITA

An Introduction to the Philosophy of Yoga

Tom McArthur

THE AQUARIAN PRESS
Wellingborough, Northamptonshire

First published 1986

To the memory of
WILFRED ARTHUR CLARK

British Library Cataloguing in Publication Data

McArthur, Tom
Yoga and the Bhagavad-Gita: an introduction to the philosophy of yoga.
1. Yoga
I. Title
181′.45 B132.Y6

ISBN 0-85030-479-2

The Aquarian Press is part of the Thorsons Publishing Group

Printed and bound in Great Britain

Contents

Preface

This book offers no advice whatever about sitting in the lotus position, standing on your head, or controlling your breath. It says little or nothing about diet, keeping fit, or learning to meditate. It does not propose to lower anybody's blood pressure or raise anyone's kundalini. It is, however, a book about yoga, and about the primary textbook of yoga in India, the *Bhagavad-Gita*.

The first and larger part of the book deals with the evolution, nature, purpose, and paradoxes of yoga, while the second part is a complete version of the *Gita* in relatively simple modern prose. At various points in the first part there are also excerpts from and descriptions of such other original texts as the *Upanishads*, Patanjali's *Yoga-sutras*, and the *Puranas*. Both parts deal with what has always been a central issue—if not *the* central issue—of yoga and other mystical systems: the idea of 'integration', of increasing the unity of one's personality, of feeling 'at one' with the world, and of becoming a more fully awake human being. You can read the two main parts of the book in any order you wish.

The present form and content of *Yoga and the Bhagavad-Gita* has emerged out of that period of the 1970s when I ran various courses and seminars on Indian philosophy, religion, and yoga for the Department of Extra-Mural Studies of the University of Edinburgh, often in collaboration with the Scottish Yoga Association. Many people took part in those courses and seminars, helping me to frame the issues more clearly in my own mind. Among them I would like to acknowledge in particular Patricia Bramah, George Chalmers, Violet Henderson, Margaret Hendry, Helen Hogg, Feri McArthur, Patti McTavish, William Mowat-Thomson, Ian Scorgie, and Jane Thomson, for all their help, advice, support and encouragement. Margaret Hendry and Feri McArthur are specially to be thanked, for their help in creating the final shape of this book.

PART ONE
THE QUEST FOR INTEGRATION
Yoga and Indian Philosophy

1.
An Antique Word

Siddhartha saw it and smiled.

'Bend near to me!' he whispered in Govinda's ear. 'Come, still nearer, quite close! Kiss me on the forehead, Govinda.'

Although surprised, Govinda was compelled by a great love and presentiment to obey him; he leaned close to him and touched his forehead with his lips. As he did this, something wonderful happened to him. . . .

He no longer saw the face of his friend Siddhartha. Instead he saw other faces, many faces, a long series, a continuous stream of faces—hundreds, thousands, which all came and disappeared and yet all seemed to be there at the same time, which all continually changed and renewed themselves and which were yet all Siddhartha. . . . He saw the face of a newly born child, red and full of wrinkles, ready to cry. He saw the face of a murderer, saw him plunge a knife into the body of a man; at the same moment he saw this criminal kneeling down, bound, and his head cut off by an executioner.

He saw the naked bodies of men and women in the postures and transports of passionate love. He saw corpses stretched out, still, cold, empty. . . . He saw Krishna and Agni. He saw all these forms and faces in a thousand relationships to each other, all helping each other, loving, hating and destroying each other and becoming newly born. Each one was mortal, a passionate, painful example of all that is transitory. Yet none of them died, they only changed, were always reborn, continually had a new face: only time stood between one face and another.

And all these forms and faces rested, flowed, reproduced, swam past and merged into each other, and over them all there was continually something thin, unreal and yet existing, stretched across like thin glass or ice, like a transparent skin, shell, form or mask of water—and this mask was Siddhartha's smiling face which Govinda touched with his lips at that moment.

You may or may not recognize this quotation, but whether you do or do not it will nonetheless set all sorts of bells ringing. It is clearly oriental, certainly sufficiently so to make one wonder if it is a translation.

It *is* a translation, by Hilda Rosner, but not from Sanskrit, Hindi, or any other Indian source. Instead, it is a piece lifted bodily from near the end of *Siddhartha*, a tale about ancient India written in 1922 by the German novelist Herman Hesse. It is therefore a paradox: an integral part of German literature while also being profoundly Eastern.

Hesse is only one of many Westerners who have written—and written well—about India, using Indian philosophy, Buddhism, and yoga as a vehicle for discussing the ultimate problems of life. He is part of a tradition that dates back two hundred years, during which, for example, one single Hindu book has been translated into English by at least fifty people with at least fifty different ways of presenting it to their public. That book is the *Bhagavad-Gita*, a powerful echo of which one finds in what Govinda saw when he kissed the dying Siddhartha's brow.

Fifty is a remarkable number of translations and versions of just one book, while books on aspects of oriental philosophy and mysticism published in the leading Western languages must number in the thousands. So much time and enthusiasm lavished on making sense of an East to which the West so recently sent missionaries, soldiers, and administrators and now sends economic advisers and aid-givers. Has it been worth all that effort? Can there really be a panacea out there, as many Easterners would themselves like to believe—a counterbalance to 'Western materialism' and 'the Death of God', a key to the other hemisphere of the brain, a map of the other side of the psyche? Or is that all just so much wishful thinking, misplaced hope in a land of dirt and poverty, the homeless sleeping in the streets of Bombay, and emaciated sacred cows blocking the flow of modern traffic?

Many people look to yoga as a kind of Eastern promise, but there are in fact a variety of good reasons, apart from an interest in health or mysticism, for studying yoga and its background. For example, the very antiquity of the subject. There are precious few human traditions that extend in an unbroken line through thirty centuries or more—effectively from the Bronze to the Space Age—without losing their ability to attract, alter, or simply con a multitude of people. That is success on a quite remarkable scale, and we can legitimately ask how something so strange could possibly be so successful.

There are no Egyptian pharaohs now, but when Cleopatra lived there were yogis, and there are yogis still. The Greek philosophers and the Roman legions are no more, the Arab-Muslim expansion has come and gone, and the European maritime empires on which the sun wasn't supposed to set have all been dismantled. Some kind of yoga was there when all that was happening, and many kinds of yoga are here now—some even being considered for use aboard starships. When the god Zeus was being worshipped in Dodona and Christ walked in Galilee there were gurus teaching their pupils under bodhi trees, and there are still gurus teaching their pupils under such trees. *That* is continuity, and it is worth a little thought.

The scale of the enterprise is also worth a little thought. As a subject, yoga is embedded in the literature of the Hindus as well as in their age-old practices, and that literature is in turn one of the richest seams of recorded language anywhere on the planet. The sheer volume of stories, treatises, and commentaries challenges the imagination. For example, the 112 Upanishads alone are equal in length to the Bible, while Vyasa's *Mahabharata* with its 100,000 verses is so extensive that Homer's *Iliad* and *Odyssey* could be lost in it about seven times over. After these two collections, one comes to Valmiki's *Ramayana*, the *Puranas* and the *Agamas* before moving out of properly 'classical' times—and earlier than all of these are the four strange prehistoric works, the *Vedas* themselves, hardly read at all today but viewed by traditional Hindus as the source from which all else has flowed.

The much-translated *Gita*, a poem of 700 verses organized in 18 short chapters, is simply one book in the vast *Mahabharata*, which is a romantic epic of kings, queens, gods, demons, heroes and villains, magicians and marvels already over a thousand years old before Malory wrote about King Arthur or Spenser penned his *Faerie Queene*.

Another, final reason for being curious about yoga could be the odd quicksilver quality of both word and idea: it can seem like all things to all seekers, as the following claims-cum-definitions suggest:

- When the yogi has full power over his body then he obtains a new body of spiritual fire that is beyond illness, old age and death (*Svetasvatara Upanishad*, *c*.2,500 years old).
- Yoga is controlling the ripples of the mind (Patanjali's *Yoga-sutras*, *c*.2,000 years old).
- Yoga is not for someone who eats too much or does not eat at all, who sleeps too much or does not sleep at all. It is for the person who knows a middle way in eating and in resting, in expressions and in actions, in sleeping and in waking—and this yoga destroys all pain (*Bhagavad-Gita*, over 2,000 years old).
- The aim of the doctrines of Hindu philosophy and of training in yoga is to transcend the limits of individualized consciousness (Heinrich Zimmer, 1946).
- Yoga is a science which teaches how to awake our latent powers and hasten the process of human evolution (Swami Vishnudevananda, 1955).
- The practice of yoga induces a primary sense of measure and proportion. Reduced to our own body, our first instrument, we learn to play it, drawing from it maximum resonance and harmony (Yehudi Menuhin, 1966).

- For many thousands of people dreams of new life, a return to second youth, a beautiful, strong and trim body which radiates health and vitality, a wonderful peace of mind, have come true through my yoga instruction (Richard Hittleman, 1971).
- It is the most complete synthesis of the realities of life and living (Howard Kent, 1977).

What can all this mean? Such statements waver between clinical calm and fervent evangelism, between helpful suggestions and commercial hype. How on earth did it come about that one ancient Indian word could contain so much, could encapsulate so many assertions and promises about health, harmony, second youth, synthesis, longevity and latent powers, human evolution and inner peace—and always, waiting in the wings, ultimate bliss in union with the Creator, Sustainer, and Dissolver of all things?

Isn't it all more than one antique word can reasonably be expected to bear?

2.

Yoking the Horses of the Mind

The word itself is a story, before we even ask how it has evolved from its roots in the Sanskrit language.

The name *Sanskrit* means 'perfected'. It was in its heyday a linguistic instrument honed to perfection by craftsmen for one supreme purpose: to convey the hymns and hopes of the brahmin caste and the peoples they represented upwards to the gods, along with the smoke of sacrifice and the symbolism of ritual. The Sanskrit language was steadily removed from the everyday world, until children still learned it from their teachers, but few used it for living conversation. You talked to the gods with Sanskrit, not to mortals; indeed, among the brahmins were the world's first phoneticians, who studied the sacred sounds to ensure that time and usage did not corrupt them. Sanskrit was the language of the 'seed' mantras, potent syllables that were supposed like AUM to encompass the universe or like KHA to cause death. In such company, one can expect 'yoga' to have been magical before it became either philosophical, or (as Swami Vishnudevananda suggests) scientific.

Nowadays Sanskrit is known to the world less as the liturgical language of brahminical Hinduism and more as the easternmost of the Indo-European language family, whose nature was identified during the nineteenth century by Western philologists. The first European to study Sanskrit systematically was Sir William Jones (1746–94), who described it as having a 'wonderful structure, more perfect than the Greek, more copious than the Latin and more exquisitely refined than either'.

As a consequence, many scholars have studied Sanskrit less for what it said or had been used for than as a quarry for word-forms with which to compare other word-forms in Persian, Armenian, Greek, Latin, Lithuanian, Russian, German, and of course English, which is one of the westernmost of the Indo-European languages.

Such investigations, however, have had the curious effect of demonstrating that the exotic nasal chants of the brahmins and the words enshrined in devanagari script are kin to most of Europe's languages, far nearer to them than Samoan, Sioux, or Swahili. Indeed, Sanskrit could hardly be alien at all if *mata* was 'the same' as *mater* and *mother* and the fire-god Agni was just 'ignite' and 'ignition' in another form. The *Vedas* proved in such analyses to be philological kin to the Greek 'idea' and Latin 'video', meaning metaphorical sight or knowledge; while *atman*, that puzzling word for self or soul, was close cousin to the first element in 'atmosphere', and had originally meant no more than the breath of life and wind in the trees.

'Yoga' is just such a long-lost cousin. Its root or base in Sanskrit means binding or yoking. It is cognate with the Greek *zygós* which gives us 'zygote' in biology and with the Latin *jugum*, the yoke that lies behind 'conjugal' and even 'jugular' (from the shape of the human collar-bone).

Where English and Latin, however, restricted 'yoke' to what you did with oxen and slaves (and figuratively with marriage partners), Sanskrit extended 'yoga' to the very limits of human thought. The process was complex, but began with a race who called themselves the Aryas or Noble Ones. They migrated down into the great northern plains of India from the Hindu Kush, Iran, and central Eurasia during the second millennium BC, probably in waves and trickles like the pioneers on the North American plains in their covered wagons. They were warlike nomadic clansfolk, sure of themselves and determinedly contemptuous of the Dravidian peoples they found in the plains of the Indus and the Ganges rivers, where they steadily usurped power over several centuries, much as the Norman aristocracy did in the British Isles but on a far vaster scale.

They disdained the locals as *Dasas* or slaves, frowned at their dark skins and flattened noses, curled their lips at the cult of the penis, and destroyed or avoided such cities as Harappa and Mohenjo-daro that had been flourishing for at least a thousand years, with efficient plumbing and baths, and a commerce that reached to Babylon. Whatever merits their new subjects might possess dawned on them only slowly, not unlike what happened thousands of years later in the British Raj.

The Aryas were a heroic and patriarchal society who worshipped sky gods, made lavish sacrifices, drank an intoxicant juice called soma, organized their clans into tight social classes, studied their dreams and the omens around them, and valued the martial arts, cattle, and horses. Skill obsessed them, whether in conducting hymns and rites with meticulous care or in the use of bow and arrow, horse and chariot. They were socially exclusive, but some among them more so than others. The brahmins, who insisted on their social pre-eminence as men who ensured the coming up and going down of the sun, kept to themselves, disliked intermarriage, and jealously guarded their family knowledge, which was in due course organized in a number of *Vedas* or books of insight. The kshatriyas—governors and warriors—were less exclusive but equally proud; they were the literal cutting edge of the invasion, and learned to admire the skills of other warrior élites with whom they came into contact and conflict. Intermarriage and the conferring of kshatriya status on darker folk than themselves were acceptable to them. And in the process, they appear to have developed some at least of the early ingredients of yoga.

Although the kshatriyas conceded the religious primacy of the brahmins, they conceded little else. They were just as interested as any brahmin in questioning the nature of reality and searching for better tools for coping with life. Religious metaphor is vivid in the scriptures of the Aryas, and it is often bluntly martial:

- Take the great bow of the Upanishad and place in it an arrow sharpened by meditation. Draw the bow with concentration upon THAT and hit the centre of the indestructible target (*Mundaka Upanishad*).
- Know that the self is lord of a chariot and the body is that chariot. Reason is the driver, and mind the reins. The horses, it is said, are the senses (*Katha Upanishad*).

This is the basic physical, mental and social climate in which the word and the idea 'yoga' developed. The *Katha Upanishad* goes on to state that someone who does not understand the nature of things properly and whose mind is never steady does not govern his own life; 'he is like a bad driver with wild horses'. But somebody who understands things properly and whose mind is always steady is governor of his own life; 'he is like a good driver with well-trained horses'.

The same heroic symbolism is shared by both the *Upanishads* and the *Bhagavad-Gita*, which is probably the single most popular and influential work of Hindu philosophy and religion, either inside India or abroad. It was compiled some two thousand years ago, long after the Aryan invasion was forgotten, but the story that it tells was already old, much as Homer's tale of Troy was old when he composed it—set in a mythic age of kshatriya princes ranged in two armies upon a great and ominous field of battle. The two speakers are seated in a chariot between the opposing hordes—and the teacher is the dark-skinned charioteer, the pupil the fair-skinned Aryan prince. Worse, the charioteer is God incarnate, the Lord Krishna himself, while the irresolute prince is Arjuna, a hero of the Pandava clan. Krishna holds the reins and keeps the horses steady while he explains—of all things—Prince Arjuna's caste duty to him. The *Gita* is a poem replete with all sorts of ironies operating on many levels, not the least of which is racial.

At first sight horses, chariots and harness as a metaphor for self-control might seem alien and irrelevant, while a battlefield is no place at all to locate a treatise on the transcendental, but this conclusion might be too hasty.

Firstly, the idea of harnessing or binding is not entirely alien to the West: it underlies the word 'religion' itself, which contains the same root LIG ('binding') as *ligament* and *ligature*. Presumably, just as a ligament holds bone and cartilage together, so religion is binding on its followers. So, traditionally, the dedicated yoga student is bound to guru and goal, seeking all the time to become a *yukta*, one who is properly harnessed, trained or focused, and so—paradoxically—free.

Secondly, the West is not without its own literature of war blended with religious ideals, and may well have derived this literary style and the ideals of chivalry that go with it via the Arabs from India. Many centuries later than the Hindu epics, the stories of Roland, Percival, Gawain, Arthur, Galahad, and the Holy Grail are replete with knights in shining armour on gaily caparisoned steeds, riding out to rid the world of evil and gain salvation for themselves and others. They are also full of magic, miracles, and marvels, just like the old stories of India, and reflect a similar feudal-heroic society where priest and knight were not always comfortable in each other's company.

From the yoking of horses, the word 'yoga' extended to include the team of beasts and then the vehicle that they pulled. It extended to the equipment an army used and the use to which the equipment might be put: to performance, action, getting things done, to devices, stratagems and tricks, even to magic and to fraud. In the sense of a bond, it came to mean contact, combination, connection and union, while in its sense of purposefulness it extended to occupation, acquisition, profit, fitness, effort, endeavour, and zeal. And in relation to the mind, it became concentration or focus, systematic speculation, and the union of individual with universal. A quite extraordinary term, in fact, whose associated terms were legion, ranging from the word for fixing arrows in a bowstring to the word for getting married. The ancient Aryas, however, could never have imagined how far both word and idea would go, when they first yoked horse to war-cart and then speculated about the disciplining of body, mind and spirit.

3.

Shamans and Demon-Kings

Cholchinay was beautiful, and loved the hunter Choril. Soon she would braid her hair into two plaits and marry him. Whenever they looked at each other they were happy—but someone else was also looking at Cholchinay and licking his lips with desire.

Allykh the shaman already had ten wives of his own who cared for his every need. They even chewed his meat for him, so that all he had to do was swallow it; but none of this was enough. He wanted Cholchinay too.

Allykh was a powerful man. Twelve brasses hung from his belt, and twelve shamans had worn those brasses before him. His powers were great, and now he used them to conjure up a snowstorm that would start the winter early and bury Choril while he was out hunting. When the young hunter lost his way in the storm, however, he came across the den of a she-bear, explained that he meant her no harm, and snuggled beside her for warmth. He grew sleepy, like the bear, and couldn't rouse himself, while the voice of the Master of the Mountain whispered in his ear: 'Whoever sleeps with a she-bear through the winter becomes a bear.'

Meanwhile Allykh told the people that Choril was dead, and claimed Cholchinay. He said he would care for her till she was ready to braid her hair and become his eleventh wife. Throughout the winter he kept urging the marriage on her, but she would not give in to him, and when the spring came took Choril's weapons and fled into the wilds to look for him.

Cholchinay found the den of the bear, and out of it came a tall, handsome beast that looked as though it would attack her. She used Choril's weapons on it, but they would not kill the bear, and soon she learned to her surprise and joy that the creature was her lover, Choril. They talked, and plotted the downfall of the powerful shaman, because as long as he was alive, Choril would remain a bear. Choril also told Cholchinay that every shaman had his own demon in a pot kept by the Master of the Mountain. If that demon was caught and killed, Allykh would die, and they would not have the blood of their kinsman on their hands. A bear, however, could not go to the Master of the Mountain, so Cholchinay had to undertake the task, and after some fiercesome adventures on the way she found both Master and pot, enlisting the Master's sympathy.

'Look into the pot,' he said. 'Many shamans' demons live there, and I don't know which is Allykh's. Call on it to serve its master and grab it when it comes out.'

When Cholchinay called Allykh's demon a black worm jumped from the pot. She caught it tight, thanked the Master, then climbed astride her spear and flew back to Choril. When the two of them met Allykh again he was furiously searching for her, and was very surprised indeed to see Choril. Before he could recover his wits, however, Cholchinay dropped the black worm to the ground and stamped on it before the horrified shaman's eyes. He died when it died, the bearskin slid from Choril's back, and the pair were free to marry, forget Allykh, and live a long and happy life together.

Which is not an Indian story at all, but a folk-tale that still goes the rounds among the hunter-gathering peoples of Eastern Siberia. In their world, magic is still of the essence of things, while the village shaman or medicine man is—or was until very recently—a powerful, valued, but feared local figure, awesome and in direct touch with both good and evil spirits.

Shaman is a Siberian word that in English means 'one who knows'. Kinds of shamanism can be found all over the world among so-called primitive people, actively at work in Africa, Haiti, and Brazil, or surviving in pockets and patches elsewhere. The English word *wizard* also means 'one who knows', and quite possibly *witch* is the same (cognate with having quick *wits*). The *Vedas* or books of knowledge show that the brahmins reckoned they 'knew', inspired by ancient *rishis* who could see and hear what ordinary folk could not see or hear. Even in the relatively late *Bhagavad-Gita*, *jnana* or 'knowledge' means special knowledge, and someone who is truly aware is called 'the one who knows'. The Persian *magi*, who gave their name to 'magic', were also people who had special knowledge and are still called Wise Men in Christian tradition.

Such sorcerers have also always had their apprentices, as witnessed by the twelve brasses at Allykh's belt. Initiator and initiant in turn had handed those brasses down, and raw power with them. In more sophisticated eras and societies the laying on of hands can be done gently and be called an 'apostolic succession', but underneath the veneer of gentility and rationalism the old obsession with special knowledge and skills is still there. The tale of Cholchinay, Choril, and the Shaman still strikes a common chord.

Shamanism is, in terms of our civilization, a relic of the Stone or at best the Bronze Age, important to people like the tribes of the Amur in Siberia or the Sioux in North America. It is entirely committed to the world of nature, plants, animals, human survival, and ceremonial power in the clan. Shamans might or might not be clan leaders, but whether they were men or women they were all charismatic, uncanny, jealous of their powers, and inclined to engage in psychic duels with their rivals. They were purportedly chosen by the spirits and had the power to heal or harm, bless or curse, change shape or change nature. They could only be defeated with their own weapons, as the Siberian story demonstrates.

One reason for introducing the Siberian tale at this point is that several scholars of repute, including Mircea Eliade and Georg Feuerstein, have argued that there is a link between yoga and shamanism. Another and related reason is to compare the story just told with one of the great stories of ancient India, Valmiki's epic *Ramayana*.

The *Ramayana* is far longer and more complex than the tale of Cholchinay and Choril. It comprises seven books, totalling 24,000 verses, and was put together about 2,400 years ago from much older oral material. Like the larger epic, the *Mahabharata*, it tells of how the god Vishnu descends into human form in order to defeat evil and restore the balance of the cosmos. In this instance, his consort Lakshmi descends with him and they become the prince Rama and his devoted wife Sita. The purpose of the double incarnation is to defeat the demon-king Ravana, who has gained such enormous power that the gods of the *Vedas* are useless against him. Ravana is so potent a sorcerer and warrior that he has made his enemies incapable of acting directly against him, and so a subterfuge is necessary. A true god or *sura* can only defeat this anti-god or *asura* by approaching, as it were, from the wrong direction: as an apparent mortal without a hope of winning. The bait for the trap is Sita, so beautiful that the demon-king eagerly abducts her to his island fortress of Lanka.

Rama and Sita win, of course, and live more or less happily ever after, whether they are mortals or descended gods. Traditional Hinduism adores them both and has set them up as ideals of morality, the perfect man and woman, husband and wife—role models for all. The parallels between this vast ancient story and the brief but alluring Siberian tale are startling, and could be pushed further. Choril becomes a bear after having been sheltered by a bear; Rama is helped by whole armies of monkeys and bears. Sita resists the blandishments of Ravana to the end, ever faithful to Rama, just as Cholchinay resists Allykh despite his fearsome powers. Other potent beings come to the aid of Rama in the nick of time, just as the Master of the Mountain helps Cholchinay—and of course Ravana like Allykh can only be beaten by using his own tricks against him.

Let us look at the final duel between Rama and Ravana. The invasion of Lanka is bloody and difficult, and at last the demon-king is forced to defend himself directly against his persistent enemy. The Vedic gods, watchful but unable to intervene, send down to Rama a special chariot belonging to the warrior-god Indra himself and driven by the master charioteer Matali. Rama boards it, taking with him a sword and two quiverfuls of magic arrows.

The battle that follows takes in both earth and sky and consists in equal parts of martial prowess and magic arts. Each throws a variety of dire things at the other, Ravana at one stage, infuriated, conjuring up by means of a weapon called Maya ('illusion') a phantom army of warriors already slain by Rama's legions. This almost unnerves the prince, but he struggles on, finally drawing out the Arrow of Brahma from his quiver, a dart known for its ability to destroy monsters but to be used only when all else has failed. Chanting and concentrating, Rama invokes its fullest powers and hurls it not at Ravana's head but at his heart, where he is known to be vulnerable. When the *asura* worked upon the invulnerability of his several arms and heads, he forgot about the core of his being—where the deadly *Brahmasthra* now enters.

Rama watches Ravana fall headlong to the earth from his chariot. As he dies, the demon-king is transformed by the burning strength of the prince's weapon. Layer after layer, pride and rage, ambition, greed, lust and egotism are seared away from his inmost essence, leaving his true nature exposed to Rama's sorrowful gaze. Ravana's constant meditation upon Rama, even with the intention of destroying him, has borne psychic fruit, and when the *asura* dies he is at peace.

A whole spectrum of points can be noted here—as with most Hindu stories. Firstly, the tale is more moral and didactic than the Siberian story: there is hope even for the most evil demon, once he has been overcome with the weapons of faith, concentration, and white magic. Secondly, we are out of the cold northern forests and back once more in a world of chariots, warriors, bows and arrows. Thirdly, the epic *Ramayana* blends a warriors' duel with both a sorcerers' contest and the great battle between light and darkness, good and evil. It is St George and the dragon transposed; indeed, it is *Star Wars* without moving to another galaxy.

Fourthly, it is an allegory built, apparently, upon the wars between Aryans and Dravidians, in which the Aryans have the greatest possible respect for the skills, weapons, and inner strengths of the enemy. And finally, it is more than warfare or magic. It is religious philosophy built on to, or interwoven with, popular story-telling in a most efficient fashion.

The combat between Rama and Ravana is just as much a treatise on yoga as the *Bhagavad Gita*, which is one reason that—twenty-three centuries or so later—a non-violent swami from Bengal could call himself Ramakrishna and start a mission that went far beyond India. Rama and Krishna, as avatars or incarnations of the god Vishnu, embody certain of the oldest concepts of the warrior-yogi—now forgotten or superseded in literal terms and seen as symbolic of life's general struggle. Rama and Krishna, ancient heroes of the kshatriya caste, remain for most Hindus guides and gurus *par excellence* in the art of yoga.

4.
The Fires of Asceticism

As we have seen, the yoga tradition is embedded in myth and magic. For some, that lends it additional charm, for others the mythic and the magical only strengthen their scepticism, because surely nothing serious can be founded on fairy tales about sorcerers and flying chariots?

Carl Gustav Jung has, however, suggested that human beings have two ways of thinking and responding to the world around them: a directed, rational, cause-and-effect way on the one side, and a diffuse, intuitive, fantasy mode on the other, a tendency that will not go away no matter how hard we prod it with the goad of reason. Even if we banish its poetry from our waking lives, it flourishes in our dreams, where we can't root it out. Indeed, logic, rationalism and the scientific method are fairly recent acquisitions of the human race—fragile cuttings hardly yet grafted on to the tough old stock that we loosely call 'superstition'. Superstition was all our species had for hundreds of thousands of years, and somehow we have survived because of or in spite of it. That anything as ancient as yoga is rooted in 'superstition' and the 'supernatural' should therefore come as no surprise.

In the Western world, logic stands on one side and myth on the other. Objective analysis and measurement, controlled experimentation, statistics and natural science are all immensely valuable; indeed, they were as valuable to the ancient Hindus as to the classical Greeks. Hindus as well as Greeks used such hard everyday tools of the mind as mathematics, logic and grammar, but it is worth recalling that Aryabhata in the fifth century AD first wrote about *pi* in a poem; the two ways of seeing things, the logical and the poetical, are not necessarily hostile to each other just because in our modern world few physicists are poets and few poets are physicists.

India has a continuity in its civilization that the West lacks. The gods of Greece and Rome have gone, preserved only in art and children's storybooks—but the gods of ancient India are still worshipped and their myths used by adult and child alike. An outside religion, Christianity, moved into Western Europe and displaced almost everything that was there before; although Islam and Christianity have similarly entered India, they never succeeded in usurping the central role of Hinduism, and were indeed slowly altered by it. The Western world had a Renaissance and a Reformation, in which it slowly moved away from Christianity; nothing of this kind happened in India until the late nineteenth century, and a hundred years later Westernization has still not essentially altered the traditional ways of thinking and behaving in the subcontinent.

As a consequence, although modern India has heavy industry and space technology, it also lives within the same continuum as Gautama the Buddha and the compiler of the *Ramayana*. The story of a saint alive today takes on the texture of myth almost as you watch. Whether he wanted it or not, Mohandas Karamchand Gandhi became in the eyes of his followers first a yogi, then a mahatma, and finally an avatar of the god Vishnu, on a par with Rama and Krishna in the epics. Accounts of a present-day wonder-worker like Satya Sai Baba sound like those of Swaminarayan in the nineteenth century, Guru Nanak in the sixteenth, Ramanuja in the eleventh and so on back to Patanjali, Yajnavalkya, and the primordial Rishis. They all belong in the same unbroken fabric of a timeless kind of history where dates and centuries are not central issues at all.

The special powers or *siddhis* belong in the same climate of thought. Only a very Westernized Hindu doubts the special powers of yogis and saints, or denies that they are as possible today as three thousand years ago. In Hinduism, the age of miracles is not over and cannot in the very nature of things be over. As a consequence, what the yogic tradition has to say about the *siddhis* is for Hindus entirely authentic. About them Patanjali, the most clinical and cryptic of the ancients, said:

> The siddhis are obtained either as a birthright [from a past life], through herbal means, by means of chanting, by asceticism, or by the power of concentration. (*Yoga-sutras* 4:1)

He was crystal-clear on just what these powers are: yogic concentration, for example, can lead almost matter-of-factly to the understanding of animal sounds, a knowledge of one's past lives, telepathic understanding, invisibility, knowledge of when one will die, vast physical strength, remote vision, resistance to hunger, omniscience, awareness of supernatural beings, ability to resist the very blandishments of the gods, halo-formation around the body, levitation, flight, and the indestructibility of the body. In other words, the whole bag of sorcerer's tricks.

Patanjali's *Yoga-sutras* are as widely read today as ever they were, possibly more outside than inside India. Non-Hindu enthusiasts about yoga, reading Patanjali, have to come to terms somehow with those frequent statements—banner headlines indeed—about what the adept can achieve along the path to *samadhi*. One cannot, however much one might like to, walk around these statements, nor can one dismiss them as prehistoric twaddle, if only because they make up such a large part of such a small book as the *Yoga-sutras*. Patanjali's ladder to liberation, the curious psychophysical discipline that he described and recommended, was and is a challenge to nature itself and a manual for the acquisition of personal power greater than that possessed by the greatest king. Swami Vivekananda (1862–1902) summed the matter up succinctly when he wrote:

> According to the Raja-yogi, the external world is but the gross form of the internal, or subtle. The man who has discovered and learnt how to manipulate the internal forces will get the whole of nature under his control. The yogi proposes to himself no less a task than to master the whole of nature. He wants to arrive at the point where what we call 'nature's laws' will have no influence over him, where he will be able to get beyond them all. (*Raja-Yoga,* 13)

Which is what the shamans and demon-kings wanted, what the witch-doctor and the alchemist have wanted, and even in their own ways what the monk and the priest, the philosopher and the scientist want: power over nature, so that they will no longer be her puppets and her victims. Like shamanism, alchemy, priesthood, and science, the technology of yoga concerns first and foremost an ascending line through security and prestige to worldly power and then to the same power as the gods were supposed to possess. In ancient times, as the story of Ravana suggests, such power was neutral, and could be used for good or for ill, for egotism or altruism. There were techniques, and they could be followed, and if followed successfully, the master of those techniques could wring whatever he wanted from the gods in their heaven. He could render them powerless to stop him, no matter what he might plan to do.

In present-day terms, one might say that both Adolf Hitler and Albert Schweitzer had charisma, but whereas Schweitzer used *his* charismatic powers for good, Hitler used his with the full panoply of the demon-king. Given a tradition in which enemies of the *Vedas* and good order regularly acquired and then misused vast paranormal powers, it is no surprise that later generations inculcating yoga stressed the need for a firm ethical basis before the *siddhis* were acquired.

Hindu sacred texts abound in stories of the use and abuse of powers acquired by what appears to have been a kind of self-torture. The stories of demon-kings who were always kings but not always entirely demonic date from the centuries when the Aryan tribes were learning to co-exist with the aboriginal Dravidian peoples of the subcontinent. The Aryas, with their established gods and sacrificial rituals, slowly accommodated themselves to indigenous schools of thought and action, but in their scriptures tell the story as though it were the Vedic gods and not themselves who had to do the accommodating. In other words, when the Aryas told stories about what happened to their gods, they were telling stories about what once, long ago, had happened to themselves.

Foremost in these tales is a figure who is not quite demon and not quite god, a wild and supernatural hippie with matted hair, an ambivalence between the ascetic and the erotic, and such uncanny powers that right up to the present he has been known as the *Mahayogi*, the Great Yogi. He is Shiva, a shadowy and destructive figure who in later centuries became the supreme deity of many sects and one of the classical trinity of Brahma the Creator, Vishnu the Preserver, and Shiva the Destroyer who dances the dance of dissolution within a circle of flame. Shiva had no avatars, never fought in princely style from a chariot, and had no proper place in the caste system of gods or men. His partner was and still is the great goddess with such names as Parvati or Kali, and many stories are told about their cosmic romance. Here is one, that highlights the whole complex relationship inside Hinduism between the erotic on one side and the ascetic on the other.

Yet another demon threatened the order of the world, and yet again the Vedic gods were powerless against him. This time it was clear that they needed the help of Shiva, whom they had earlier rejected and reviled as an uncouth barbarian. Reluctantly, they asked Parvati to search for him and unite with him once again, because only a child born of their union could save the world from the monstrous energies and ambitions of this new assailant. The Great Ascetic, however, had found existence too painful when, long ago, he had lost Parvati in tragic circumstances; unable to endure this loss he had retreated to the summit of Mount Kailas in the Himalayas, where he sat in a deep trance from which nothing could rouse him.

Parvati decided that the only way to rouse Shiva was to use yoga upon the yogi. So she sat down before him, composed herself, and endured the blazing sun in summer and the icy blast of winter, along with the rigours of hunger and thirst, until the inner power that she accumulated in this way penetrated to Shiva's inmost being.

At last he opened his eyes, smiled, and congratulated her. The moment this happened, her wizened form filled out and her devastating natural beauty returned, so that Shiva desired Parvati once again and balance came back into the world. The gods' hopes were then fulfilled, and in due course the demon was defeated. Incidentally, this strange tale indicates that yogic asceticism was not the sole preserve of men in those far-off times. Parvati's attendants were known as *yoginis* (female yogis), which shows that then as now yoga was accessible to both sexes, although there has always been a general assumption in India that it is a masculine concern.

People accustomed to the gentle elegance of Westernized yoga in a club or gym hall inevitably find it hard to understand and appreciate rather savage and virtually prehistoric tales like these. Such tales, however, remain crucial to an understanding of how yoga has evolved, and how its present-day techniques—whether physical, mental or spiritual, or all three together—derive from a remote and harsh regime of self-imposed torment indulged in mainly by men whose normal pastime was warfare.

The standard word for the ascetic rigours of Shiva and Parvati is *tapas,* which basically means 'heat' or 'fire'. The ancient Aryas were fascinated by fire, as were their cousins the Zoroastrians of Iran, who worship it to this day. Fire purifies, whether in religious sacrifice or in the smelting of metals; the more heat, the greater the purification. Agni the god of fire had two faces, one benign, the other malign—just like Shiva. *Tapas,* however, was less concerned with external fire (and the male and female firesticks with which it was produced) than with an inner fire that the early yogis associated with breathing (which can easily be compared to the bellows used in a smithy). This was the force that they particularly wanted to harness and which they have always conceived as basically sexual.

In later times, it has been symbolized as running through the *nadis* or channels of the body (whether physical or subtle is unimportant), and ready to rise like an awakened serpent from where it is coiled near the genitals. This latter is the now-famous *kundalini*, 'serpent fire', of *hatha-yoga* and *Tantra*—movements which reached their height during the Middle Ages. It is a complex and sophisticated theory of the workings of the body, mind, and spirit, and in all likelihood derives from the self-mortification in which many Hindu yogis and fakirs have engaged since time immemorial. *Tapas*, in consequence, means not just heat or fire but also torment, penance, austerity, and the kind of self-mutilation that was also once practised in early and medieval Christendom, when men became celibate, sat alone on high pillars, whipped themselves, and wore hair-shirts.

The bed of nails therefore has its place in yoga, however much it may embarrass purists who feel that it debases the subject. Much of the past of the subject belongs to enormously stubborn men who stood for days on end upon one leg, held one arm above their heads until it could no longer be used, and so forth. The early yogis were inveterate experimenters upon themselves, and slowly over unrecorded periods of time must have developed, in the course of their excesses, rigorous practices that did pay off in a variety of ways. Among these, were techniques for cleansing the body and binding it to the will, so that sexuality, eating, drinking, sleeping, salivating, urinating, and defecating would not get in the way of concentration and the acquisition of a clearer vision of life, prestige, power and — inevitably—what lay beyond them all. The manipulation of the body may have begun at this time, although there is no direct evidence that it did, and in all probability one of the factors at work in such manipulation was moulding the human frame so that it resembled the stances of certain admired animals. The many postures named after animals—cobra, locust, scorpion, lion, and the like—cannot just have sprung out of chance resemblances. Yogis in the forests and mountains had plenty of time to watch cats stretching and snakes rearing up.

The essential aim, however, was manipulation of environment as much as self, and this can best be illustrated through the story of King Bhagiratha. A prince of the Vaivasvata clan, Bhagiratha claimed direct descent from the sun itself. The sun, however, had become all too powerful, blazing down in a terrible drought that was slowly destroying everything. It was necessary to bring this drought to an end, and only the king could do this. He therefore committed his kingdom to the care of his ministers and went to Gokarna, a place that was sacred to the uncanny demon-god Shiva. Here, Bhagiratha had a fire lit to his immediate north, then one to his south, a third to his east and a fourth to his west, while the fifth fire, the sun, continued to blaze down from above. He then for an eternity of time practised *panchatapas*, the penance of the five fires, concentrating his mind and calling upon the gods to heed him.

And of course the gods had to heed him, because the power created by this fervent asceticism was irresistible. They gave Bhagiratha what he wanted, which was nothing less than the diversion of the Holy Ganga, the river of heaven, down through Shiva's matted locks to the slopes of the Himalayas and thence across the plains to the sea. In this way, the earthly river Ganges was born, and the terrible drought brought to an end.

This idea of the voluntary ordeal in which one creates an inner fire so strong that the outer world can be changed is still widespread in India —as, incidentally, is the belief that holy men can act as rain-makers. Mahatma Gandhi was an ascetic of the old school who had a technique that he called *satyagraha* or 'truth force'. It lay at the core of his political activity, in the acts of passive resistance and the fasts through which he sought to alter the behaviour of others. Indeed, he used this ascetic force on two particular targets: the enormous and well-established empire of the British in India, and his own followers and fellow nationals when they did not behave as he wanted them to behave. His *satyagraha* is the basis of a kind of direct non-violent political action common in many parts of the world today. It requires great self-discipline and a willingness to suffer; it appears to be passive, but is in fact virulently active on the minds of others, as Bhagiratha's penance was active upon the gods. What is more, in Gandhi's case most Hindus see it as successful. First of all, it got rid of the British, as he promised, and secondly, some Hindus feared its success so much that they arranged to assassinate the Mahatma rather than see him go on to use further *satyagraha* to change their way of life and make them live at peace with each other and with the Muslims. Killing him was a perverse compliment that acknowledged the strength of his *tapas*.

5.
Vibhuti

The trouble with the *siddhis* is that they will not go away. They cannot be rationalized out of yoga by means of some tidy modern Western process of sanitization. They are an integral part of the traditions, not just a legacy from a remote magical past, not only an on-going interest in a 'supernatural' now more comfortably called the 'paranormal', but also a challenge thrown down with an inscrutable smile at strict materialism and scientific scepticism. It is a challenge which cannot be ignored.

Whenever the subject of yoga comes up in general conversation someone brings in the special powers: Can yogis *really* go into states of suspended animation, levitate, and what have you? The ensuing speculation provides a field day for the sceptical and the credulous alike: the sceptics because at the end of the discussion they can have a good laugh, and the credulous because at the end of the same discussion they can feel their faith reinforced. Both win, because both fought the battle on their own ground.

As a consequence, the subject is generally whatever you want it to be. Fortunately, however, there are a few pointers to matters that demand more than simple-minded faith or equally simple-minded disbelief. I would like to take a look at three such pointers now, embodied in three separate but interlinked reports.

The first two are particularly interwoven and belong to the time when I lived and worked in Bombay in the 1960s. At the time, various yogis, swamis, and sadhus were in vogue, and the newspapers enjoyed reporting on two particular figures who seemed about to engage in the kind of psychophysical duel that shamans enjoy and Rama and Ravana experienced.

The first of these was a hard-core exponent of yoga as a discipline founded on the body: Hatayogi Laxman S.Rao. He looked perfect for the part: elderly but lean, hard and fit, with a gaunt handsome face, piercing eyes, a hawk-like nose and a long white beard—almost a cliche' of the archetypal yogi. The second was so different he was comic relief, a chubby South Indian with a penchant for long saffron gowns. Shri Satya Sai Baba looked more like a carnival figure than the godman acclaimed by his followers. Plump to the point of being cuddly, he had a Lou Costello face in which the eyes looked out with benign calculation—and an Afro hairstyle like a black sunburst round his head.

I must admit I was biassed from the start. I greatly preferred the austerely dignified hatha-yogi, and disapproved heartily of the funny man and his bag of supernatural circus tricks. So too did Hatayogi Rao. In April 1966 he issued a public challenge to Sai Baba on the front cover of *Blitz*, a Bombay tabloid that enjoyed setting cats among pigeons. It read:

> I, Hatayogi L.S. Rao, challenge Shri Satya Sai Baba to produce currency notes, diamond rings, watches, mangalsutra, kumkum, flowers and bhasma in my presence. If he demonstrates and produces it I will put all my spiritual and material wealth, except my soul, at his feet and become his chela for life. If not, I expect him to reciprocate the gesture.

The epic contest did not, however, ensue. Whether the Baba's continued public success in—apparently—materializing these items in front of open-mouthed devotees galvanized him or not, the Hatayogi some weeks later in June announced his own show, in which he promised to perform a selection of the miracles of his craft before an invited audience of notables and others willing to pay for the privilege of attending the open-air suburban performance. I could have got a ticket and gone, but did not feel that the outlay of a hundred rupees—no small sum—was justified.

Hatayogi Rao's performance took place, and was widely reported in the local press and abroad. For starters he chewed and swallowed nails and what was said to be nitric acid then, none the worse for the hors-d'oeuvre, walked across a bed of hot coals trailing behind him a towel that caught fire. He was unharmed, and went on to the *pièce de résistance*, which was a specially prepared tank of water about five feet deep. He climbed to the edge, stepped on the smooth surface of the water—and sank like a stone. Press photographs showed with admirable impartiality the hatha-yogi first walking on fire and then soaked in the tank. Triumph became disaster, and later he was reported as saying he would return all money taken from the sale of tickets, and that he had failed because he had sunk so low as to charge an entrance fee.

Satya Sai Baba, as far as I know, made no public comment on the humiliation of the man who had hoped to humiliate him. I did not have the opportunity to see or meet the Baba—and had no great desire to do so, assuming that his reputation would be as open to deflation as the hatha-yogi's. Towards the end of my stay in India, however, I stated in an article on Hinduism in the magazine *Opinion* that I had talked to a South Indian colleague, a man from Kerala, about the wonder-working Sai Baba. He had told me he was himself a religious sceptic, but knew a family of devotees to the Baba who possessed three pictures of him. Around these pictures, he said, entirely seriously, accumulated a sacred ash that he called *vibhuti*, and after a certain point the *vibhuti* would drip off. The ash came from nowhere, he said, a gift at a distance from the Baba to his devotees.

I did not believe my Keralite friend, but I asked him if I could see this wonderful telekinetic ash. Certainly, he said; it could be arranged, but it never *was* arranged, though I politely asked again—and again. It was never quite convenient, and my own picture of Sai Baba, which I had bought with a wry smile, hardly even gathered dust.

Part of my reason for mentioning the matter in the article (entitled 'The Perplexities of Hinduism', October 1967) was that I rather hoped some reader out there might respond to it, just to show this sceptical fellow what was what. And somebody did, a Konkani lawyer who worked not far from Cathedral School, where I worked. His name was S. K. Nadkarni, and he wrote: 'I do not pretend to be a follower of Satya Sai Baba but this miracle you refer to I have seen. . . . Firstly I had gone to satisfy my curiosity and on two other occasions I had taken some friends to show the miracle.' He offered to do the same for me, I went to meet him in his office, we agreed a time, and met again one Friday evening in November.

First we went to Dadar, where a lady was waiting to act as guide, evidently not to the house he knew, but to another, in the district of Matunga. To my surprise, I already knew the lady, who was the mother of one of my students, Narayan Arur, a Westernized lad who would have been highly embarrassed by the whole thing if he had known about it. We whisked off in a taxi and drew up in due course in a dingy street of tenements occupied mainly by Madrasi families.

We entered a ground-floor apartment, in the living room of which pictures of both famous Sai Babas were prominently displayed. I should mention here that the earlier one, Sai Baba of Shirdi, a small lean ascetic figure much loved by Bombay taxi-drivers (who often carried a photo of him at the time), had died many years earlier, and that the second Sai Baba claimed to be his reincarnation. Be that as it may, however, quantities of light grey material were clearly adhering to the pictures. The elderly widow who was head of the small family had no objection to my closely examining them. What I saw was, firstly, a large framed picture of the smaller, older Shirdi Baba, in the lower right-hand corner of which was a small superimposed print of Satya Sai Baba. The seated figure of the earlier saint was bare, but the other was covered in ash so thickly as to constitute a kind of doughnut or ring covering the Afro coiffure, leaving the face exposed. I assumed right away that the devotees kept the face clear of the stuff. On the second picture, a new and larger one of Satya Sai Baba, little clusters of ash were scattered here and there like grey lichen clinging to the glass.

The room was rather bare and drab, not too well lit, and the effect was eerie. Everyone else had gone on into the kitchen, leaving me there, then came drifting back. I was nonplussed, quite content that I had now seen what I had wanted to see, but the others treated all this business in the living room as trivial. Mr Nadkarni smiled and insisted that I should now come on into the kitchen. I supposed that some kind of hospitality was in order, and ducked through into the longish, narrow kitchen area, typically bare and austere. But in that typically bare and austere kitchen there was far more to be seen—a whole wall shrine to the two saints, *and that whole wall almost covered in ash.*

Perhaps seven square feet of ordinary plaster wall was white-grey with *vibhuti*, giving off a sweetish temple smell. The ash was spread between a large number of scattered pictures of the saints that were hung on nails or arranged on small low shelves at knee height. Some bowls of water stood on these shelves, where a lone agarbatti stick burned—shedding hardly enough ash to cover a pinhead. I made as careful an examination as I could, the others respectfully holding back to give me plenty of room. The widow's eldest daughter spoke English, and said:

'When we first became devotees of Baba, we put the pictures here and the walls became covered with *vibhuti* in the shape of the Shiv-lingam. This was important for us, because we are a Vaishnav family which did not worship the lingam. This was a sign of Hindu unity which Baba gave us.' She then pointed to a large picture of a standing figure, again Satya Sai Baba, although only the face acted as a means of identification, because the whole figure in the picture was concealed in a red mass that had accumulated on the glass—also in the shape of the Lingam. 'This is *kum-kum*. It came here like the *vibhuti,*' the girl added.

The face in the lingam reminded me of similar motifs I had seen in temples, museums, and books.

'Do you keep the face clean?' I asked.

She smiled diffidently, obviously eager to get it all right for the European, possibly the first she had ever talked to.

'No. We do not touch the pictures. And we do not touch the *vibhuti* till it falls from the pictures.'

There was enough *vibhuti* collected on the shelves and the bottom rims of the picture frames to provide *prasad* for a long queue of devotees. I was told that the day before had been the Baba's birthday and a crowd had come to celebrate it. They had taken large quantities of the ash as *prasad*, and yet there was an abundance left. I looked closely at it, but was not rewarded with any evidence of spontaneous generation. However, it was clear to me that anybody conducting a pious fraud would have had to spend a lot of night-hours sitting up and sticking ash (brought from where, in these quantities, of this fineness?) on walls and pictures—hardly a pastime for the sane and quite without profit, as these people did not obtain a paisa from the possession of so strange a shrine. Certainly, they asked me for nothing.

'Why does the *vibhuti* form here?' I asked.

'Baba makes the *vibhuti* form in certain places which can be centres for his followers.'

'Do you know any other place?'

'There is one in Santa Cruz.' Yes, that was probably the one my Keralite colleague knew about.

'I heard of a man who carried a small picture of Baba in his pocket and the *vibhuti* appeared there,' somebody said.

'There was a person who was a devotee of Shirdi Baba and went to a meeting of Satya Sai Baba,' said someone else in the crowd. 'When she looked at Baba, she did not see his face at all—only Shirdi Baba's.' This to reinforce the reincarnation claim. Meanwhile, the old lady was pouring *tirth* from the bowls on the shelves into the cupped palms of the various people now present. They drank it down.

'This is tap-water only,' said the girl. 'Camphor comes in it like the *vibhuti*.'

I was offered some, and smelled the camphor, but refused it, more in awe at that moment of Bombay's risky tap-water than transmogrified camphor.

'Would the lady give me some *vibhuti*?' I wondered.

'Yes. They are happy to give it.' My guide implied that they had to dispose of all that largesse somehow.

I was therefore supplied with small slips of folded paper containing *vibhuti* and *kum-kum*, which I later handed over to our head chemistry teacher at the school, without explanation, asking for an analysis. Not surprisingly, they proved to be *vibhuti* ash and *kum-kum* powder. I have a small phial of the ash to this day, kept in a drawer of my desk.

With typical Hindu grace, my guides expressed full belief in the miraculous nature of the thing without confessing themselves to be devotees of the Baba. In fact, this both Mr Nadkarni and Mrs Arur denied; it was not for them. As we drove away, however, after thanking our hosts, the lawyer said that the matter was clearly a miracle, but what did *I* think? I said that it was remarkable, altogether strange, but I would need to have the room sealed off for at least forty-eight hours, and guarded by reliable people, having measured the ash—somehow—before locking the shrine. Then one could check it with proper, scientific precision. If fresh ash appeared under such conditions, I could make a positive statement of acceptance.

'That is unnecessary,' smiled Mr Nadkarni. 'Too complicated. You see and believe. That is enough.'

'You aren't afflicted with a Western mind,' I answered.

But I was grateful for his kindness in taking me to that street in Matunga and to the edge of something that was entirely uncanny. I said so in due course in *Opinion* magazine, on 9 January 1968, and the above account is drawn more or less word for word from my account there, which was based on notes I made as soon as I got home that evening. I offer no further comment here, except that I haven't the slightest idea how the unseen baba pulled it all off—and that the name for ash, *vibhuti*, also happens to be a synonym for *siddhi*, the commoner word for any power beyond the normal.

Western science is slowly coming to terms of a sort with yoga and the yogis. Thus, Marion Wenger of the University of California at Los Angeles and Basu Bagchi of the University of Michigan Medical School travelled to India in 1957 and studied the claims that yogis could stop their hearts by taking special deep breaths, holding such a breath, closing the windpipe, locking the chin against the chest and contracting the chest and abdominal muscles. With little or no blood to pump, the heartbeat faded, but EKGs revealed that the organ was still contracting and expanding, even if the beat could no longer be heard.

Further research showed that one yogi could bring his heartbeat down from a low 63 to a graveyard 24 beats per minute without relying on muscle control, evidently by putting pressure on the carotid sinus, a set of receptors sensitive to changes in pressure. According to Dr Bal Anand of the All-India Institute of Medical Sciences in New Delhi, this might have been achieved by increasing the firing of the vagus nerve, which is linked to the autonomic nervous system and inhibits rhythm.

Dina Ingber in her report 'Yoga the Impossible Science' (*Science Digest*, February 1981) describes these and other more recent studies. Among them she includes a report in the *American Heart Journal* in 1973 that a yogi was buried for eight days, his vital signs monitored throughout. After twenty-nine hours, his heart rate increased sharply from 106 beats per minute to 250, after which his EKG showed 'a straight line with no electrical disturbance', which continued unbroken for the next six days (no one disturbing the body!). On the eighth day, half an hour before the pit was to be reopened, the EKG record started up again, and the yogi revived on schedule.

Dr Neal Miller's theory and practice of biofeedback runs parallel to yogic ideas and rests on the assumption underlying Patanjali's *Yoga-sutras* that, in Ingber's words, 'we can learn to control almost any bodily function if we can become aware of it'. Control of one's muscles is easiest, because the feedback is immediate and visible; making other less accessible bodily activities as visible, Miller reasoned, might make them as easy to affect. He consequently developed machines which people could use as aids to becoming aware of heart rate, blood pressure, and brain waves at work. By making a light go on or a beeping sound go away—willing this to happen—Miller's patients could will changes inside themselves, and possibly a lot more quickly than through traditional yoga. Patients find it hard to describe what is going on when they make such changes; many, however, say that they 'visualize' what they want to happen and in due course, if they concentrate on their visualization, it happens. Such visualization is, among others, an ancient yoga technique.

Currently we are only on the doorstep of the possibilities hinted at by the various hybridizations of Western science and Eastern yoga. However, the hunt is on, as can be seen from the kind of articles now being published in the review of the Indian Academy of Yoga, headquarters Banaras Hindu University, India, an organization of scientists and scholars interested in yoga and of yoga practitioners interested in science and scholarship. Article titles from review issues in recent years include 'Yoga and psychosomatic illnesses', 'Effect of selected yogic asanas and physical exercises on flexibility', 'Mental health and yoga', 'Physiological benefits in hatha yoga training', 'Cardio-respiratory changes during savitri pranayam and shavasan', 'possibilities of jnana yoga therapy for psychosomatic diseases', 'Study of respiratory functions during Kapalbhati', and so forth. And now that the hunt *is* on, it is hardly likely to be called off. The results are altogether too interesting.

Scientists at present can cope—just—with altered heart rates and blood pressure reduced by visualization techniques, although these are radical matters. They are hardly yet willing to look at the other matters that are just as important in Patanjali's tradition as breath-control and suspended animation. Levitation, invisibility, telekinesis, and—if my *vibhuti* appeared the way the believers said it appeared—some kind of matter transmission or materialization of molecular structure out of nowhere. Well, these are still some distance away, to be discussed in science fiction but not in science fact. They are in fact still in the realm of 'magic' where of course they may well remain.

And yet . . . Hatayogi Rao failed to walk on water, but he *did* walk on fire in front of many witnesses, unhurt while his trailing towel burst into flames. And the ash in the phial in my desk drawer had to come from somewhere, somehow. An EKG machine is a hard-edged artifact of the material world, and if it reports that a yogi's heartbeat dissolved into a 'straight line with no electrical disturbance' for six days, then one must pay some attention, unless of course one would just rather not know.

6.

The Eternal Law

Can one study French cooking without wanting—and needing—to know something about France and the French? Similarly, can defensive arts like *judo* and *aikido* be separated off from the Japan in which they developed? It might be argued that for a relatively superficial dip into *haute cuisine* and *aiki-jujutsu* one can get by with a few words from the mother language while concentrating on technique. For a fuller study, however? It may not of course be possible to go to France or Japan, but nowadays the subjects themselves have emigrated and *cordon bleu* courses and *dojos* are widely available elsewhere, as are plenty of commentaries and translations in well-brought-out books.

Yoga is comparable, and practitioner-investigators whether Western or Eastern generally agree about the extent to which yoga and India are intertwined, an understanding and appreciation of the one requiring an understanding and appreciation of the other. Two quotations can serve to illustrate this point:

> The supreme role played by yogic practices in the maintenance of mental health and efficiency has been known to mankind for centuries. In fact, it can be stated without any doubt that yoga is the most important contribution by Indian culture to mankind. The entire fabric of Indian culture over the past many centuries has been woven round the concepts of yoga. (B. Ramamurthi, 'Mental Health in Yoga', *The Yoga Review*, Spring 1983: Quarterly Journal of the Indian Academy of Yoga)

> The word *yoga* refers to that enormous body of spiritual precepts and techniques which grew up in India over several millennia and which may be regarded as the very sub-stratum of the cultural life of Indian man. (Georg Feuerstein, *Textbook of Yoga*, Rider, 1975, p.3)

But how to come to terms with India, and in particular with the kaleidoscope of Hinduism? Perhaps, first of all, by divesting it of some of the unnecessary assumptions about it. It is at first—and second—glance a welter of texts and sects, schools and schisms, profound truths and perplexing illogicalities, *but* it is no more reasonable to look for simplicity and clarity in Hinduism than to expect to see straight away the common thread uniting the Vatican State in Italy with the Radio Church of God in California, the Bible Belt in the southern USA with Holy Week in Seville, the Salvation Army in England with the Copts of Egypt, the Quakers of Pennsylvania with the Mormons of Utah—or an Anglican tea party with the misogynistic republic of monks on Mount Athos in Greece.

Indeed, if all the forms of Christianity from voodoo in Haiti to Christian Science in Boston were penned up—and had for centuries been penned up—in one peninsula, however large, then the results would be much the same as the Hinduism we see today. Vishnu and Shiva are no more at odds than Calvin and the Papacy; the Hare Krishna movement and the Ramakrishna Mission are no further apart than the Pentecostalists and the Jesuits.

Hinduism is India's response to what the German philosopher of religion Rudolf Otto has called 'the numinous', that mystery all around us that fascinates and inspires awe. The universe into which we are born—thrust, thrown, whatever, weak and dependent as kittens—is only ever partly explicable, often hostile, and always awesome, whether we want to feel the awe or not. No amount of cliché can diminish an object of such immense natural grandeur as the Grand Canyon or the Ganges, and no amount of hiding can keep disease, old age, and death out of sight forever. The numinous seeps into our lives at every point; it is never more than a sunset or a traffic accident away.

Nobody could ever have thought up so grand, baffling, splendid, sordid, and stupid a world as the one we live in, and throughout our lives we have to *cope*, somehow, with both the grandeur and the mess, whence the attraction of any system—magical or scientific—that offers to enhance our security, prestige, power, and understanding, even slightly. This truism is as true in the West as the East, the present and the past. Worse, it will be just as true again tomorrow.

Most dictionaries define *awe* as an emotion compounded of such other emotions as dread, reverence, and wonder. It can elate or it can depress; it can separate us from everything around about and make us feel tiny, puny, and futile; or it can overwhelm with a warm pantheistic sense of unity, in which you embrace the cosmos and the cosmos embraces you right back. Like most of us, the Hindus have preferred the embrace—the sense of unity and belonging—to the feeling of dread and separation. Unlike the rest of us, however, they have built much of their culture around 'ladders' between the messiness of every day and making permanent the feeling that they call *ananda* or bliss. They have supposed for centuries that somewhere far away but also right beside us is a place where that bliss is *the* permanent condition.

What the whole human race appears always to have wanted is a belief system that allows both communication and communion between the Human and the Aweful, assurance and insurance against the dark and the cold. It appears to have emerged in relation to seven evolving and interlinked areas of experience:

Firstly, in terms of vast natural events that are beyond human control and defy easy explanation, such as thunderstorms, earthquakes, flood, pestilence, and both the good and the bad harvests.

Secondly, in terms of particular wonders of nature, such as mountain ranges and major rivers, or one unusual mountain and one unusual river, such as Olympus and the Ganges.

Thirdly, in terms of a conviction that 'others' exist, whether they are friendly, hostile, or indifferent to human affairs. These others are as natural as ourselves, and never go away; they need acknowledgement, which could be placation, coercion, coaxing, deception, reverence, worship, sacrifice, or prayer. They cannot be ignored, whether they are conceived as deities, devils, nature spirits or beings from Unidentified Flying Objects who were the First Astronauts and will Come Again. Importantly, such Others are capable of physical or figurative sexual intercourse with us, so that changelings, monsters, demi-gods, or messiahs can come into existence. In present-day Western secular civilization it is fashionable—and for many of us entirely justifiable—to play down this aspect of the numinous, but in terms of the bulk of history and much of the human race today, the view that God is dead is still a minority view.

Fourthly, we acknowledge—however reluctantly—certain favoured groups of humans, chosen, self-chosen, or divinized. These include the brahmin caste, the Nation of Israel, any of the Elects of Christ at any time, the Roman Catholic priesthood or any other ordained priesthood, certain dynasties of rulers with celestial ancestry such as the imperial family of Japan, or until recently with divine right, such as the British royal family. Such groups persist, despite opposition (indeed, almost thriving on it), and cause all kinds of personal, racial, and religious tensions over whether their claims are true or their privileges earned.

Fifthly, we acknowledge—grudgingly or with holy joy—certain charismatic individuals who are seen as either the divine descending into flesh or the human ascending to godhood. These persons can range from shamanistic mouthpieces of the spirits to incarnations like Christ the Son of God, the avatars of Vishnu, or the Manifestations of God proposed by the Baha'i Faith. In addition, they can also be perceived as self-realized practitioners of such technologies of liberation as yoga.

Sixthly, certain artifacts of our own species gain a sacred quality, whether they are holy collections of writings like the Bible, religious buildings like the cathedrals of Europe or the mosques of Islam, or sacred cities like Jerusalem, Rome, Mecca, and Benares.

Seventhly, and finally, all or any of these factors blend into a social fabric called a 'religion', of such compelling strength that it becomes itself an object of reverence and loyalty, the vehicle of a god or gods and a means by which individuals can locate and identify themselves. They then know what they should be, who they agree with and are therefore acceptable to (the faithful, the Elect) and who they do not, can not, and must not agree with (the infidels, the ungodly).

Hinduism demonstrates the interplay of the seven factors over at least three thousand years. Natural disasters are a constant in the collective Indian experience, part of the Wheel of Rebirth. Mountains, rivers, cities, and shrines have all been turned into focuses of supernatural power; they are the *bindus* or 'points' where the gods meet us or this world touches the Other. Hinduism has a vast array of deities from several contenders to the supreme rank, through local and village godlings to a god-like priestly caste and a whole galaxy of men who become gods and gods who become men.

Hinduism combines in its gigantic tapestry the threads of both fantasy and logic, where some centuries ago the Western world severed the two fairly thoroughly. In the West, rationality and fantasy live uneasily together in divided minds; in India at large, the division was never even attempted, at least not until the coming of European education. As a consequence, Westerners in India who wish to understand the background against which they move are forced into an imaginative adjustment of the kind that one meets in the novels of Herman Hesse, E.M. Forster, John Masters, and Robin White. Students of yoga have to do the same; the subject cannot be lifted out of the social, religious, and symbolic matrix in which it has evolved and continues to evolve, and cannot be successfully described without using many of the technical terms transmitted down the centuries.

Because of its vast complexity, Hinduism is inherently perplexing and its philosophies inherently paradoxical; indeed, this is part of their strength. They won't tamely co-operate and fit; they tease the mind and force it to go further. The moment you think you have grasped a concept, pattern, or subtle point, something else comes along to upset the apple-cart of your (self-)satisfaction. This has to be faced at the outset. There *is* a great deal of logic and consistency in Indian philosophy and yoga, but it co-occurs—sometimes appears to be embedded or mired—in an even greater amount of illogic, non-logic, and intuition, while ultimately its essence does not depend on logic at all, disdains it, and seeks to transcend it. If one cannot accept this blend of everyday frustration side by side with the mystic's insistence that human language and reasoning are not enough, then one will inevitably have trouble with such central concepts as *maya* and *atman*.

The fundamentals of Hinduism and of yoga are about nine in number. They can be summed up as: caste and its obligations; reincarnation and its consequences; polytheism overlying and co-existing with a variety of monotheistic currents; an abiding sense of oneness behind the flux of existence; a propensity to assimilate rather than exclude; a tradition of tolerance that co-occurs with caste exclusiveness and recurrent outbursts of violence and bloodshed; a popular vision of Deity as a divine pair with an active and pervasive sexuality; a willingness to believe that the divine mingles with the human, the animal, and the inanimate, and that 'God' takes on human and other forms in order to restore the balance of things; and running through it all a stream of mystical do-it-yourself centred upon a tradition of gurus passing on a core of truth to their students, generation upon generation.

In the ebb and flow of history there is a continuum between the teaching of the cool, detached hermits and the vibrant, lyrical cults of devotees in village, city, and pilgrim centre. For centuries, Hindu thinkers of all backgrounds have debated which among the myriad of methods, often overlapping most confusingly in their ideologies and their techniques, is the best avenue to blissful release from the Wheel of Rebirth—and continue to debate and disagree. What they do tend to agree about, however, is that all ways—even the long, roundabout ways through hell—eventually lead to the same goal. That is the common ground of the *sanatana dharma*, the Hindus' own name for Hinduism—the Eternal Law.

The essence of the Eternal Law is to be found, by common agreement, in the *Upanishads*, those mythic and mystical treatises that began to be compiled around 800 BC. A blend of poetry and philosophy, they serve to distil the speculations of ancient India. They are not easy to read even in the original, and are extremely hard to translate without numerous notes and queries. The next chapter, however, with all these provisos, is a re-working of the *Katha Upanishad* in modern form, so as to give some idea of the vitality as well as the central message of the original teachings handed down from master to disciple.

7.

Nachiketas in the House of Death

The poor brahmin Ushan prepared for his entry into heaven, and paid all his cattle as a fee for the proper sacrifices. But they were a worn and milked-out lot, which made his son Nachiketas ashamed.

'Anybody who pays with beasts like that will get a poor sort of heaven in return,' he thought, and pleaded three times with his father to give him away instead. Ushan did not enjoy being reminded of his poverty, and in exasperation told his son to go to hell, to Death himself, and bother *him*.

Nachiketas did exactly that. He went down to the nether world, where he spent three nights in solemn thought without eating anything at all. He thought about death as the fate of all mortals; how we grow tall like the corn, are cut down when we are ripe, and are seeded all over again, to repeat the cycle forever. Yama the god of death was away from his home, but after the third night he came back and was horrified to see that a brahmin boy had been in his house for so long without hospitality. To ward off the bad luck, he said:

'Brahmin, you have spent three nights in my house and eaten nothing all that time. I wish you well, and ask you in recompense to choose three boons from me, any three in my power to give.'

Nachiketas was relieved to hear this, and asked as the first boon that his father's anger should have gone by the time he got back home.

'Your father will be glad to see you when you return to him,' said Yama benignly. 'Young men don't often come back from the jaws of Death, so your father will sleep all the better for your safe return. And the second boon?'

Nachiketas still had his father's sacrifice and cattle on his mind.

'Heaven,' he said, 'is a place without fear, old age and death, so they say. Tell me about the sacred fire that serves as the gate to such a heaven.'

'Certainly,' said Death, and gave the lad an account of just how the triple fire should be laid and just how many bricks should be used for the altar and where they should be put. 'The fire god takes care of everything after that. And your third boon?'

Nachiketas frowned.

'Some people have doubts,' he said. 'Some say that when a man dies there is nothing more. No future, no heaven, nothing at all. Death, tell me the truth about this. What really happens when people die?'

'Ask me something else,' said Yama, turning away. 'Anything else at all. This question of yours puzzled even the gods themselves in days gone by. It's all very subtle and mysterious. Ask for something else.'

'You alone have the answer! There is no boon more valuable to me than this.'

'Choose sons who will live for a hundred years, choose a wealth of cattle and land—long life and fame—beautiful women, chariots and song! But don't press me on this.'

'All these things pass,' said Nachiketas. 'Lord, keep the chariots and the songs, because at the end of them all you are still waiting there, aren't you? In the presence of an undecaying immortal like you how can I accept the fleeting pleasures of a long life? Death, what happens when we die? This is the only boon I'll choose, so tell me!'

Death smiled.

'If you insist, then I must tell you, but only because you have already come half the distance, brahmin boy. You have made the necessary choice, that essential discrimination between what is easy and congenial and what is hard but eternal. You rejected the temptations of wealth and ease, which most men would have gladly chosen, assured that there is just one world, the one in which they rush back and forward, getting and keeping.

'You need a teacher to take you through the barrier of ignorance. It is by no means easy to get beyond that barrier, because what lies beyond is subtler than all logic. Reasoning can't grasp *this* idea, my friend Nachiketas, but you have had the good sense to come to someone who can teach you.

'The fundamental Brahman, that is the god to think about. A wise man engages in the yoga of the primal self, the *atman*. It is hard to see, fixed firm in a secret place beyond both sorrow and joy.'

'Tell me about the untellable!'said Nachiketas. 'Tell me about what lies beyond right and wrong!'

'The Vedas reduce to a single word, and all the fire of asceticism distils into the single sound for which men practise chastity. That syllable is AUM. Understand it, and you have everything, because it is the best and highest support. This essence is not born and does not die, has not come from anywhere and has never become anybody. Unborn, steady, ageless, primordial, it is not slain when the body is slain. If the killer thinks, "I kill", or the slaughtered supposes "I have been killed", then both are wrong, for the essence neither kills nor is killed.

'Tinier than the tiniest, vaster than the most immense, the *atman* lives at the heart of all beings, where only someone without involvement can see it. Motionless it moves, bodiless among the bodies, unchanging in the midst of change, a god of both joy and joylessness. The Self is the Lord of everything, and with the mind fixed upon him the wise know no grief.

'The *atman* can't be reached through teaching, through the intellect or through being learned; he chooses you, you don't choose him. The evil and the disturbed, people whose minds are filled with restlessness—they can't grasp him, no matter how clever they are. For him, both the brahmins and the kshatriyas are just a dish of rice with death as the spice. Who really knows where he is?

'Know this then,' said Yama. 'The self is lord of a chariot and the body is that chariot. Reason is the driver and mind the reins. The horses, it is said, are the senses, and their paths are the objects of the senses. Self, reason, mind, and senses together make what men call "the experiencer". Someone who does not understand things properly, and whose mind is never steady does not govern his own life. He is like a bad driver with wild horses. But someone who understands things properly and whose mind is always steady does govern his own life. He is like a good driver with well-trained horses.

'The unmindful and the impure never reach the goal; they simply go on with birth and death. The mindful and the pure, those with understanding, reach the goal, from where they are never born again. The man who reins in his mind, with the skill of the charioteer, he reaches the end of his journey, which is the abode of Vishnu.

'There are the senses and the objects of the senses. There are the objects of the senses and the mind. There are the mind and reason. Beyond the reason is the *atman*, and beyond the *atman* is what never appears at all. Beyond that again is the goal which is unseen but can yet be seen by those who know how to look.

'A wise man curbs himself, and submits to the Self. Wake up to that fact, Nachiketas, which is as hard to cross as a razor's edge, a dangerous journey, as the bards have said. But by discerning the soundless, the touchless, the formless, the imperishable that is without beginning and end, by discerning THAT will you be liberated from the mouth of Death himself. Everything that you can ever think of, IT IS THAT. Sleeping and waking, what was and what is still to be is THAT. *Tapas* and *prana* and whatever they achieve are THAT. The sun when it rises and when it sets, and the fire in the firesticks are THAT. A bird in the sky, a god in the air, a priest at the altar, a guest in the home, the out-breath going upward and the in-breath coming downward, the body and the soul in the body, all are THAT, and for fear of it all things go their ways.

'When the five senses are stilled, then the mind is stilled. When reason no longer moves, the highest way is reached. This steadiness is yoga, the beginning and the end. When all the knots of attachment are cut, then mortal becomes immortal.

'A hundred and one currents pervade the heart, but of them all only one rises to the head. The others are dissipated at death, and only this one current leads to deathlessness. The inmost self is the size of a thumb. Draw him out like pith from a reed, and know him for what he is.'

That is what Death himself taught to Nachiketas—the whole art and craft of yoga. That is how the boy found the peace of Brahman and freedom from death, and how you may find it too.

8.

Tell Me More, Father

The *Katha* is one of the less difficult *Upanishads*, and appears to be the earliest surviving treatise on yoga. Many others followed, most of them continuing in the mythic style, with its enthusiasm for dramatic instruction by means of parabolic stories. If it were not embedded in the body of the epic *Mahabharata*, the *Bhagavad-Gita* could also be called an upanishad, whose name means 'sitting near' (that is, at the feet of one's master). The *Gita* has the same didactic features—an instructive dialogue between initiator and initiant—as well as verses that are virtually identical with material in some of the *Upanishads* (including the *Katha*).

Many present-day scholars would agree with Robert Hume when he states that the *Upanishads* were 'the first recorded attempts of the Hindus at systematic philosophizing . . . their efforts to construe the world of experience as a rational whole' (*The Thirteen Principal Upanishads*, Oxford, 1931). Certainly, the *Katha* for example displays a general discontent with the old, exclusive brahminical sacrifices (Ushan, the impoverished father) and their hypocrisies (the old, milked-out cows). The younger generation (Nachiketas, the son) nonetheless wants to maintain tradition as best it can (the offer of self-sacrifice; the first and second boons), but the new radicals will not be fobbed off with easy traditional explanations (the second boon) or the promises of earthly success (the preamble to the third boon). Instead, they want clarity of mind and the truth, however hard (the third boon, taught by Death himself).

This is typical of the revolutionary change of direction that took place around the middle centuries of the first millennium BC. It occurred both inside brahminism and beyond it, in the unorthodox anti-brahminical movements that drew their inspiration from such kshatriya princes as Mahavira and Gautama, the founders of Jainism and Buddhism respectively. The inner fire was now more attractive than the smoke rising to the sky; that inner fire rose not just to heaven but to a higher and more permanent condition that the Buddha called *nirvana*, the sunset, the blowing out of the candle of life and desire.

Negative definitions of this kind were popular: *neti-neti*, 'not this, not that' or *kha*, 'the void'. At the same time, however, there was a positive emphasis on *ananda*, 'bliss', which was also *mukti*, the achievement of independence, *moksha*, liberation or escape, and *kaivalya*, a condition of absolute absorption into the One behind and beyond *maya*, the web of the world.

To get to that state, you harnessed the beasts of the senses (*indriyas*) to the chariot of the mind (*manas*), whose driver was reason or intellect (*buddhi*). He would hold the reins (*yama*), and thus properly yoked (*yukta*), you could go forward with discipline (*yoga*) on the right path (*marga*).

The Sanskrit root for laying out a path and providing proper guidance along the way is SADH. Its derivative *sadhu* describes the straightness or rightness of the path, the unerring quality of a well-made arrow going to its target, proper obedience along the way and the virtue accumulated in the process. It is also, as a consequence, the name for a holy man travelling along such a path. Additionally, *sadhana* is what directs you to your chosen goal. It could be the gaining of power by means of spells and the summoning up of spirits, as a shaman might do, but it is also any spiritual discipline pursued under a proper master. A *sadhaka* is anybody engaged on a *sadhana*—a worshipper, a sorcerer or his apprentice, and a yogi or his pupil.

The *Upanishads* were the recorded beginning of all the systems and terminologies of yoga. They are sermon-like, but many have one or more story-frames of the kind that I built upon in my tale of Nachiketas in the House of Death. These story-frames generally concern disciples or would-be disciples going to acknowledged masters (*rishis*) and asking questions. Thus, the *Mundaka Upanishad* begins with a brief apostolic succession of sages, then an account of how the householder Shaunaka went to the last sage in the list, Angiras, for some clue about the true nature of the world. The *rishi*'s answer was categorical enough for anybody: 'There are two kinds of knowledge, as anyone who knows can tell you—a lower knowledge and a higher knowledge. The *Vedas* are the lower knowledge.'

In the *Prasna Upanishad*, six enthusiasts go to the sage Pippalada and ask for enlightenment. He makes them wait a year in dutiful chastity, austerity and meditation, then takes their questions in turn and answers each, informing them in the process that there are two paths, one that starts off south and one that starts off north. The southern path is Vedic sacrifice and worldly activity and leads in an endless circle; the northern path, diametrically different, goes to *atman* and release.

Some of my favourite stories are told in the *Chandogya Upanishad*, a long, rambling, intricate riot of mythology, ritual, didactic comment, students and masters. It describes how even the gods themselves once feared Death and took refuge in the *Vedas*. Yama however saw them there as clearly as we can see fish in the water, and so they had to flee once more, this time into the safety of the sound called AUM, which stands of course for the *atman*. Later, the brahmin boy Shvetaketu asks his father Uddalaka—who has already been taught by the kshatriya prince Pravahana ('The Vehicle Who Carries You Forward')—for an explanation of the ultimate nature of things. Among Uddalaka's answers are, to my mind, some of the finest parables in all of Hindu literature:

'Bees make honey, my dear son, by gathering the nectar of many trees and making one thing out of all those separate juices. Yet the separate juices don't know this. They can't say "I am the juice of this tree" and "You are the juice of that tree". In just the same way, all the creatures of the world—tiger or lion, wolf or boar, worm or moth, gnat or fly—when they merge into one they don't know it. That one fine essence belongs to all. That is reality, that is the self, and you are THAT, Shvetaketu.'

'Tell me more, father,' said Shvetaketu, insatiable.

'Certainly I will. Look at the rivers, my dear son, as they flow from east to west and from west to east. They all flow into the ocean, and we no longer know which river was which. In just the same way, all the creatures of the world—tiger or lion, wolf or boar, worm or moth, gnat or fly—become that one again. That one fine essence belongs to all. That is reality, that is the self, and you are THAT, Shvetaketu.'

'Tell me more, father,' said Shvetaketu, insatiable.

'Certainly I will. Bring me a fig from over there.'

Shvetaketu brought him a fig.

'Cut it open.'

He cut it open.

'What do you see there?'

'These small seeds, father.'

'Be good enough to cut one up.'

He did so.

'What do you see there?'

'Nothing at all, father.'

'Nothing at all, my dear son. The fine essence cannot be seen, but no one denies that out of it comes a huge fig tree. That one fine essence belongs to all. That is reality, that is the self, and you are THAT, Shvetaketu.'

'Tell me more, father,' said Shvetaketu, insatiable.

'Certainly I will. Just put this piece of salt in that bowl of water and come back again in the morning.'

Shevtaketu did as he was told, and in the morning his father said to him: 'Can I have the salt back, the piece that I gave you yesterday?'

But his son couldn't give him back the piece of salt, because overnight it had dissolved completely in the water.

'Sip the water from this side of the bowl,' said Uddalaka.

Shvetaketu did so.

'What is it like?'

'Salty.'

'And from there?'

'Salty too.'

'And there?'

'Also salty.'

'Throw it away then, because it doesn't matter where you taste the water, it will be salty. The salt is everywhere in the water, and in the same way that fine essence is everywhere in the world. That is reality, that is the self, and you are THAT, Shvetaketu.'

'Tell me more, father,' said Shvetaketu, insatiable.

'Certainly I will. There was once a man who was blindfolded and led to an empty place. When he got there he had no idea where east or north or south or west might be. When they abandoned him in that place he was completely lost. But another man came up to him and took the bandage from his eyes. "Your home lies that way," he said, and showed that man who was lost where he should go. And so, being a sensible fellow, he went from village to village and checked the way, and at last returned to his home.

'In just the same way a man who has a teacher to show him the way will remain in this world only as long as he needs to find that way home. That is the one fine essence which belongs to all. That is reality, that is the self, and you are THAT, Shvetaketu.'

9.

The Human Guide

In the same way that non-Hindus who are interested in yoga have to accommodate themselves to the *siddhis* or paranormal powers, so they have to arrive at some kind of decision about the *guru*.

For Hindus this is seldom, if ever, a problem. People simply agree with Uddalaka in the *Chandogya Upanishad* that a teacher is essential. No progress can be made without one, except in extremely unusual cases. In this century, only two major figures, the saintly Shri Ramana Maharshi and the yogini Anandamayi Ma, have risen to the heights without a guru from an accredited tradition. Such a guru is not just someone you admire, but someone you acknowledge wholeheartedly and who in turn acknowledges you as a student. Obedience is expected, but it is also understood that the guru will take care of his students. It is, ultimately a relationship of mutual need; the one is dependent upon the other, but the relationship can never be forced upon either.

As a Westerner and an individualist I have always had problems with the idea of the guru. Because I am a teacher myself I value other teachers, especially if they are good at their jobs, but the idea of surrendering utterly to the dictates of another human being and revering that person like a god—as is often the case in Hinduism—has never been attractive to me. Hindus would generally put such a response down to an over-healthy ego and an unwillingness to trust. That could be true, but it could also be true that for Westerners with a valued tradition of independent thought that stretches back to Socrates at least some other kind of approach may be necessary.

I became actively involved with yoga in general and the Western yoga movement in particular when I was twenty-four and living in the town of Sutton Coldfield, in the Midlands of England. This was in the early 1960s, through the direct prompting of Wilfred Clark, who at the time was the editor of the *Sutton Coldfield News* and on the edge of retiring. Neither he nor I had any idea then, when he started up his first further-education yoga class, that he would go on to found the Birmingham Yoga Club, then the Midland Yoga Federation, and finally the British Wheel of Yoga, all when most men are ready to take on nothing more demanding than a bit of gardening. Wilf didn't look or behave like somebody who could foist yoga on an unsuspecting British public, but that is what he did. And in the process prodded, persuaded and then precipitated my Persian wife Feri and me into running perfectly enormous classes in various school gymnasia in Sutton and Birmingham. I felt something of a charlatan, quite astonished by the scores of people who signed on for courses and fascinated by the potential of the subject for them and for me.

Insofar as Wilfred bulldozed me into the circle of yoga—from which I never thereafter managed to escape—and because I admire his achievement in the twenty years that followed till his death; because he always treated me like his own son and I always greatly cared for him, however far apart we often were, then I could make *namaskar* to him and say 'guruji'. But insofar as I never saw him as the gate of truth and the guide of my sadhana, he was not my guru, and in Hindu terms, because he had never himself been initiated by his own guru, he could not serve as my or anybody else's guru—unless of course he was an utter exception to all the rules. Of course, anybody who knew Wilfred in the prime of his old age, foibles and all, knows that he was an utter exception to all the rules.

The closest I came in India to a guru was two all-too-brief encounters in Bombay with Swami Niranjana Ananda, himself a disciple of Swami Sivananda of Rishikesh. Sivananda's is a school that practises *sannyasa*, renunciation of the world, but even so many people could be accepted as students and many people regard Sivananda or one or other of his well-known personal disciples as their guru. Niranjana Ananda was a most attractive man, a handsome, bearded South Indian in a saffron robe, not very tall, dark-complexioned and with kindly, humorous eyes. On our second meeting we had a long conversation, and the following dialogue is a reconstruction of much of that conversation from the notes I made as we talked.

'Swamiji,' I asked, to start off with, 'do you think that Westerners should approach yoga in a different way from Eastern people?'

He laughed.

'The approach is the same,' he said. 'For one end there can only be one approach. Since it began in the East, Westerners must accept that we have the initiative and adapt themselves to the yoga customs. It depends really upon the mental attitude.'

At that time I was particularly concerned about a variety of problems concerning the teaching of the physical postures with which yoga is particularly identified, especially in the West, and so I asked:

'Should students attempt all the *asanas*, or are there certain positions which suit some physiques better than others?'

'You only need to attempt *asanas* according to what you want,' he answered. 'You can learn twenty-five, or hundreds. Some are easier, some are harder, but one should proceed very gradually and do as many as possible. *Asanas* are after all only a means, not an end in themselves.'

'Must hatha-yoga always pave the way for raja-yoga?'

Again the smile.

'Chinmayananda says "no", but Sivananda says that it must.'

'Is hatha only concerned with the body or has it its own mental value?'

'It is always mind through body.'

'In mental training, where does hatha end and raja begin?'

'The moment you start feeling you have control over your mind, then hatha stops and raja starts.'

'Is *samadhi* an ideal which we can fulfil in this life?'

'Never hanker after *samadhi*,' he said. 'It is a natural state for a yogi and comes when it comes. It is effortless, just as there is a point when the rice is properly boiled.'

'Who is a real yogi,' I asked, 'and how would one recognize him?'

'He is a yogi who never proclaims himself to be one. It is they who take the initiative in allowing us to see that they have attained.'

Niranjana Ananda was one of the least dogmatic of yogis, and did not in fact call himself one. His words, however, are a measure of the dedication necessary in any truly Indian *sadhana*. He knew who his guru was and knew where the path led. Westerners inevitably have problems that people like him have never had and on one occasion years later, at a seminar in the University of Edinburgh, I brought several well-established teachers of yoga in Scotland together in front of an audience of more than a hundred people to discuss this and related matters. The teachers were Helen Hogg, Ian Scorgie, Jane Thomson, and William Mowat-Thomson, all of whom before or since have been involved in training further teachers. The year was 1977, and the discussion was recorded on tape. The following is a transcript of part of that discussion as it was published in the *Journal of the Scottish Yoga Association* the following January:

Tom McArthur: Do you have a guru? Do you acknowledge any person as your guru?

Helen Hogg: The answer is simple—No. I haven't a guru. I don't acknowledge a guru, because I haven't found one yet, and I don't really know if I'm looking all that hard. If people want a guru they'll want a guru. They'll know when they want one, I think.

Ian Scorgie: I've had a guru. Taking the word in its sense of someone who sheds light in darkness—which is one meaning of the word 'guru'—yes, I've had light shed in the darkness of my own ignorance. This was a person, Chandra, a brahmin (in South India). He was rather a self-centred person, and I had no particular liking for him at the beginning at all. And he was smaller than I was, so I had a superiority complex for a start! But I found that as the association progressed he became—instead of about five feet one to my five feet two—almost ten feet tall. But I probably have a lot of self-opinionated rubbish that I put out, just as he did—so I'm infected by the person I had as a teacher. But it's left to the student to sift the gems from the rubbish.

William Mowat-Thomson: My guru is a woman, Lady Mayo. I met her seventeen or eighteen years ago, and she showed me a light in my darkness, and a way of life in the yogic sense that I did not know was possible. And she's still my teacher to this very day.

Jane Thomson: Well, I think I agree with Ian. I've had various path-lighters, and various intensity of the light they shed, but I've never had a guru. I instinctively think of a guru as completely achieved, showing me the end of the path, so I've only had path-lighters, taking me a little way on.

Tom McArthur: And are you gurus yourselves?

Helen Hogg: No, I don't think so. If a guru is someone who sheds light in your darkness, then many people are my teachers. Books and swamis and my students too, who've taught me as much as anybody else. Perhaps you can also have a guru in the sense that someone shows you the way even though they don't realize they are doing it at the time. That can happen as well. But I wouldn't class myself as a guru.

Tom McArthur: The reason I asked this question of course is that many people in India consider that you can't take on a sadhana, a spiritual course, without a guru to lead you. You have to find a guru, and he has to accept you, and you have to accept him—equally. Has anyone every treated you as a guru, Ian?

Ian Scorgie: Well, I don't know if they have—sometimes, perhaps. I see myself as a very poor-quality candle, shining in a darkness, but the quality of the wax doesn't make any difference. It's the amount of flame that goes out. Over the years so many other candles have been lit around me that I'm no longer able to see the light as just my own. It's a shared light. I'm learning from the other lights around me. I can see further with their light than I could with just my own little peep, and poor-quality wax.

William: I don't consider myself a guru in the strict sense of the word, in my own mind.

Tom: Here we have four fairly well-known people who have been teaching yoga for some time in this country, and they are to some extent breaking the Indian tradition. It is normal in India for yoga to be a guru-chela relationship, teacher to pupil, but no one here particularly wants to take on the mantle of the guru.

William: I might add, if I may, that to teach yoga you must be invited by your teacher, which I was, and that to me is a guru-chela relationship. If I have people who could become teachers, then I ask them to. I don't think it is good to teach yoga unless you're invited to, by your teacher.

Tom: So this is a kind of apostolic succession?

William: Yes. My guru Lady Mayo's teacher was Swami Sivananda, and she stayed in Rishikesh with him, and I in turn went back to Rishikesh. I think the 'apostolic succession' is very important.

Jane: Do you think it's the guru or the system he originates that's important? For instance I would say, rather like William, that I'm orientated towards the Sivananda system. My first teacher, Vishnudevananda, was a disciple of Sivananda's, like Countess Mayo. I don't really recognize him as my guru, but I do carry on the system. Some of my students asked me why I taught. I don't think any teacher really wants to teach. They have to be pushed by their teacher to teach. They're told it's their duty. Maybe I have a bit of the old Scots evangelist in me, but I still had to be pushed.

Helen: I agree with William. I was asked to teach myself, by my teacher. There was a group of us started off with Jeannette Paxton, and I really got pushed into it. I don't think I was at all ready to do it, but I did it, and have learned a lot since then. I think you should ask someone to teach; they shouldn't just decide for themselves.

Ian: My first teacher's opinion of me was very low. He classed me as representative of Western materialism, and eventually he asked me to—well—go and sort out these materialistic people in the West. But I didn't. It was some years after that someone else asked me to teach yoga. Are gurus important? As light-shedders they are; people like that are important in any society. But I also tend towards Krishnamurti in this. If there is to be a guru at all it has to be one's own awareness of the darkness that is in oneself. That very awareness is a light, and so you have the in-built, do-it-yourself guru principle.

Tom: Have you ever met a yogi? And do you consider that you are a yogi yourself?

William: Yes, I've met yogis. There can be all sorts of yogis; in fact every one of you, you're all yogis. But the yogis I met in India were mainly raja-yogis, people working rather more on the mental than the physical, and in Rishikesh there was Chidananda, who would consider himself a yogi, and indeed is reckoned to be a saint of India. I was shaking at the knees when I went into his audience chamber, but the camera soon came out and everything was quite happy in a very short time. But you're all yogis, if you only really knew it, and I'm a yogi too, I suppose, heigh-ho.

Jane: No, I'm not a yogi—not that I've realized, and I may be at such a low level that I wouldn't recognize a yogi if I saw him. At Rishikesh I also met Chidananda, and I thought he was one of the most saintly men I've ever met, but he wasn't my definition of a yogi. I've met equally saintly men elsewhere who have never practised yoga techniques. Perhaps I have met a yogi, but I'm not ready to realize it, and maybe we all have, inside us, our own ideal yogis.

Ian: Yogis are of different types. There are those you might class very loosely as being 'unmounted', and there are those who are 'mounted'. As far as I'm concerned, I'm still trying to get my foot in the stirrup! But I've met people I could say were mounted in yoga, and not necessarily Indians. We should try to get away from this whole concept of a yogi being an Indian. You meet some very enlightened people in everyday living. If you can say that they are mounted, in command of themselves, and can extend this out to you, then yes, I'm a yogi. But at the moment I'm just trying to get on that horse.

Tom: Thank you, Trooper Scorgie, for the household cavalry view of yoga!

Helen: I feel a lot like Jane. I have met somebody calling herself a yogi, Swami Atmananda. Quite a few of us have met her. I'd agree with William, too, about all of us being yogis—potential yogis or yogis anyway. Everybody has the potential. Maybe we're all yogis and don't know it. I've met one or two people whom I'd consider to be yogis, but who wouldn't perhaps consider themselves to be such. There are some here (in this hall), but I wouldn't tell you who they were.

10.
The Superhuman Guide

The *Upanishads* spread over hundreds of years, and once the style was established as an intellectual alternative to the *Vedas* a wide variety of further systems developed. In fact, the second half of the first millennium BC in India could be called a matrix of system-building, when all kinds of explanations of life and techniques for handling it developed, sometimes orthodox, sometimes heterodox, sometimes in rough harmony with each other, sometimes sharply at odds.

Those that conceded a special dignity of place to the venerable *Vedas* came to be known as *astika* or orthodox, while those that rejected the Vedas as the sterile ritualism of the brahminical caste were called *nastika*. The tension behind this division probably goes back to the immemorial antagonism of Aryan and Dravidian, but it also reflects a genuine philosophical-religious concern for truth. Today the ancient disputes are largely forgotten, or overlaid with more recent feuds, but they have left an indelible mark on the development of yoga.

The *Upanishads* exhibit many of the tensions in a crude form: a certain disdain for the *Vedas* while still paying lip service to them, sharp little reminders here and there that the kshatriyas were at least as knowledgeable as the brahmins (together with stories showing priests going humbly to princes to obtain a fuller glimpse of reality). The *Upanishads* as vehicles of intellectualism, however, contained the seeds of a much more powerful schism than simply between orthodox and unorthodox, brahmin and kshatriya, although these were almost invariably added in to complicate matters. This larger schism was in itself twofold, and haunts India to this day. The fundamental issues were and are:

- Which is better, to see the world as a snare of desires and disillusionment, an ephemeral piece of nonsense from which the wise man withdraws, seeking through austere practices to escape into an altogether higher condition OR to live in that world, to take part in its joys and sorrows, but acquire the right attitudes so that one can find nirvana here?
- Which is truer, a universe of forms that rests upon a mute invisible and impersonal fundament, the Brahman, the essence of all things, OR a universe which is the awesome *lila* or play of a personal God, who cares about everybody and everything, and from time to time intervenes directly to restore the balance of things?

In crude, broad terms and regardless of niceties of doctrine, the great religious-philosophical schools of India divide on these issues, or are strung out on a continuum in which these opposing positions are the extremes. Thus, much of the *Upanishads*, a preponderance of Buddhism, all of Jainism, many schools of yoga, many aspects of Vedanta, and so forth belong in the school of the world-negaters for whom chastity is a potent tool and cool detachment a coveted goal. On the other hand, the great popular movements associated with the gods Vishnu and Shiva and the goddess Parvati or Shakti, some schools of Buddhism, some schools of yoga, and certain kinds of Vedanta do not see the world as a hopeless snare, are not opposed to *bhoga* (pleasure) accompanying *yoga* (discipline), and prefer what might be called a warm conception of the universe. In these schools one retreats towards and into love rather than towards and into passionless isolation.

Such a tension and such a continuum are not of course the monopoly of Hinduism: Islam, Christianity, and other religions have similar polarities between asceticism and devotionalism, for example, but they do not carry the split as far, because they are—generally—based upon a guaranteed fundamental agreement that there is a sole God who from time to time intervenes in the affairs of the human race. The Hindus, the Buddhists, and the Jains have split even on that—and out of their great debate has come only one shared idea: that of the Superman.

In terms of the *Vedas* and the *Upanishads*, the supermen par excellence are the *rishis*. In terms of reactionary and ultra-ascetic Jainism, the supermen are the *tirthankaras*, the 'ford-makers' who take humankind through their aloof example across the river to oblivion. Among the revolutionary Buddhists, who created a model for a 'middle way' between extreme asceticism and the everyday, the supermen are the *buddhas* and *bodhisattvas*, the self-realized ones whom the Hindu gods envied for their freedom. For the followers of classical yoga, and the many movements that stem from it, the superman is the *yogi*, properly harnessed for the spiritual journey and at last liberated into the sublimity of stillness. For the devotional movements based on Vishnu and his manifestations Rama and Krishna, the superman is the *avatara*, very God descended to live among us and help us attain to His Presence. And so it goes on, with every possible permutation and compromise among the various standpoints. Yes, says one, buddha and avatar are in many ways the same; no, says another, they are entirely and forever different. Not at all, says a third, it is only a quirk of language and symbolism which makes us see the descending god as different from the ascending man; if we only knew, we are all gods and part of God. What is the word 'God', says a fourth—simply a crutch of language and symbolism to help people on their way; the truly free do not need such words as 'God' or 'Vishnu' or 'Brahman' or anything else to express the inexpressible.

The idea of the Superman holds fast, however, despite all the dialectic. It proposes still another continuum, this time from the lowest, meanest, grossest of humans up a ladder with many rungs to the luminous *mahatma* ('great soul') at the top. The ancient alchemical theory of the *gunas* is often used to describe how such a gradation is possible. The whole world, as the *Gita* for example insists in its closing chapters, is a fabric woven from the three great threads called in ascending order *tamas*, *rajas*, and *sattva*. As you improve yourself across many lives you slough off the dark and heavy *tamas* first, then little by little the fiery passionate *rajas*, until you consist mainly or entirely of light, ethereal *sattva*. Even that, however, is ultimately a bond and must be escaped from.

It is impossible, however, to think of the Superman—East or West—without asking questions about power. Whether it is the power of the guru over the chela, the power of the illuminated one who can burn the impertinent to cinders at a glance (as Shiva the Mahayogi once shrivelled Kama the love god), it draws us back to the primeval magician and the military men who wanted total control. Among the Jains, the kshatriya enthusiasm for the truly great transferred its admiration from the warrior in the field to the non-violent tirthankara who was also called the *Jina* or conqueror. In the legends of Buddhism, the father of Gautama the Buddha-to-be knew from the birth signs that his son would go either of two ways—to become a world-conqueror through military prowess or a world-conqueror through spiritual strength. The king preferred the first, of course, but destiny had other plans. Gautama gave up all martial ambitions for a higher and surer kind of heroism. Echoes of this ancient choice between physical bloody battle and a higher warriorhood, the Superman's, can be found still, as for example in Gandhi's war through non-war, or the following extract from a poem by Swami Vivekananda:

Let darkness go, the will-o'-the-wisp that leads
With blinking light to pile more gloom on gloom.
This thirst for life, for ever quench; it drags
From birth to death, and death to birth, the soul.
He conquers all who conquers self. Know this
And never yield, Sannaysin bold! – Om Tat Sat, Om!

(From 'The Song of the Sannyasin', composed at the Thousand Island Park, New York State, July 1895)

The *Bhagavad-Gita* is a kind of centrepiece for all Hindu thinking, in that it was composed at the height of the tensions between the old and the new, the Vedic and the Upanishadic, the brahmins and the kshatriyas, the orthodox and the heterodox, the worldly and the otherworldly, the ascetic and the domestic, the involved and the uninvolved, the attached and the detached, the world-negaters and the world-reconcilers, the seekers after an impersonal Brahman and the devotees of a personal God. It is, in essence, a work of integration in the face of social disintegration as well as a work that sought to show how people—all people, everywhere—could integrate and rise with the help of the Superman rather than watch a rare and intellectual élite save themselves through practices without meaning for the mass of humanity. Whoever composed it, its genius lies in the number of compromises it makes without dissipating itself entirely. It operates on a plethora of levels: the immediate social issues of its day; all humanity everywhere and at any time; and each individual at the sharp point of decision. To achieve its end—harmony and broadening the base of the Elect—it took an ancient martial tale and infused it with permanent philosophical worth.

The *Gita* is probably Hinduism's most popular and most widely read—and used—book. For many it is the word of God and not to be questioned any more than a devout Muslim questions the *Quran* or a devoted Christian fundamentalist questions the Gospels. Many scholars, however, have subjected the *Gita* to critical assessment, and have found it all the more interesting for that, just as they have learned things about the Gospels and the *Quran*. Like other scriptures, the *Gita* has a variety of internal inconsistencies and oddly arranged elements, contradictions on the textual level quite distinct from the paradoxes which are part of its intent. It survives its irregularities, its repetitiveness and its now-remote background, however. The whole is greater than the parts.

Perhaps the first paradox about the *Gita* is its status in Hinduism. The truly orthodox accept the *Vedas* and the *Upanishads* as *shruti* or revealed truth, but do not include either the *Gita* or the epic *Mahabharata*, in which it has traditionally been set, in that category. These are later artifacts and belong to *smriti* or tradition. Many broadly orthodox Hindus, however, and particularly the followers of Vishnu-Krishna, have felt uncomfortable about this. They want proper honour to be paid to their supreme deity and to what they see as his supreme revelation. Long ago there were only three 'proper' *Vedas*, and only slowly was a fourth added, apparently grudgingly as the brahmins accepted into their fold the lore of indigenous priests. Following this lead, the Vaishnavas or followers of Vishnu have proposed a fifth or 'lost' Veda, of which the *Gita* is an integral part, and this they call the *Itihasa-veda* or the Veda of Stories. Largely this proposal is rejected in legalistic terms, but on a wider canvas the Vaishnavas long ago won. Hardly anybody reads the original *Vedas* now, whether they offer lip service to them or not, and few read the *Upanishads*—but multitudes base their lives on the *Gita* and it is the Hindu work on yoga that most interested Westerners would like to understand (whence the fifty or so versions in English alone).

Dating the work is not easy. We know that it is later than the early *Upanishads* and the lifetime of Gautama the Buddha, who lived in Bihar in the sixth century BC. Internal evidence provides the clues here, as for example the *Gita's* use of the term *nirvana*, which is incorporated but at a suitably lower level in its own scheme of things than the level given to it by the heretical Gautama. It equates nirvana with Brahman, which Buddha did not do and would not have wanted to do, and in the process brings the *Upanishads* and Buddhism into a new and tactful alignment—part, if you like, of Hinduism's counter-reformation against the protestant under the bodhi-tree. Both nirvana and Brahman in turn are shown to be less interesting and efficient than a new ingredient called *bhakti*—loyalty and love towards a sympathetic deity—that has no place in either of these earlier systems. *Bhakti* may, of course, have had an ancient history as a popular cult of the subcontinent, but it is entirely absent in the intellectual life of the Jains, Buddhists and other ascetic movements that flowered around the sixth century BC, although as we have seen there are traces of the idea in the *Upanishads*.

Gautama the Buddha was a prince who taught that the world is a place of misery, and that we should seek escape from the wheel of birth and death called *samsara*. The Jains taught an even more extreme doctrine (that Gautama practised in his first attempts at enlightenment) and urged upon everyone as much asceticism as they could bear. Their goal was and is total inactivity, to the extent of sitting still and starving to death, in order to escape the minute flecks of *karma* that are drawn to settle on the true self (*jiva*) whenever activity takes place. The *Gita* is resolutely opposed to such extreme asceticism—the fire of *tapas*—and takes care to define proper *tapas*, a more moderate regime. More than the Buddhists the *Gita* supports a middle way between extreme rejection of this world and passionate involvement in it, and this is particularly clear in the famous description of yoga in Chapter 6:

Alone in a secluded place the yogi puts himself in harness, controlling the mind, having no hopes and possessing nothing. He takes up a steady seat in a clean place, not too high or too low, with a cloth or a hide or some grasses on it. There he sits and makes his mind one-pointed, restraining his thoughts and senses. Quite still—his body, neck and head all in an upright line—he fixes his gaze on the tip of his nose. He sits—stilled, fearless, continent, controlled, harnessed, intent on me. A yogi like that reaches the peace of my nirvana . . . The yogis who control their thoughts and discipline themselves in this way are like a lamp that stands quite steady in a windless place (See pp. 93–4)

This is, at first glance, a total compliment paid to traditional yoga, but it is the peculiar fascination and deviousness of the *Gita*'s message that all is not quite what it seems, and even such a moderated and acceptable yoga is not the best there is on offer in Krishna's universe.

11.

Questions on a Battlefield

It is just possible that there were, once upon a time, a real Krishna and a real Arjuna, involved in a historical battle of Kurukshetra in a civil war that really did take place between the Pandavas and the Kauravas over the kingdom called Hastinapura, where Delhi now stands.

If there was a kernel of historical truth then it all happened around 1000 BC, and is as hard to get at as the truth about Achilles, Agamemnon, and the siege of Troy. What is more, the Hindus don't care either way because they have never had a linear sense of history. Where the West, China, and ancient Egypt have placed an emphasis on knowing who did what and when, the Hindus have tried a bit of that now and again but much prefer to extract the juices from the harvest of the years and turn a thousand kings into Indra the king of the gods and a thousand wars into Kurukshetra or the war between Rama and Ravana. The other face of history is myth, and that is the face that Hinduism has always preferred. So, in an eternal symbolic sense it doesn't matter in the least whether Krishna and Arjuna sat in their chariot between the hostile battle lines ten thousand years ago or the day before yesterday—because Krishna and Arjuna sit in their chariot at this very instant, in the core of everything that happens to anybody.

However, all that apart, at least for the moment, we can say with fair confidence that the *Gita* was compiled within the thousand years from 500 BC to AD 500, but in all probability nearer to the first date than the second, and if it was not compiled that early then certainly all the components existed at that time.

The name means something like 'The Lord's Song' or 'The Song of the Adorable One'. The word *bhagavata* (*bhagavad-* in compounds) covers anything that is worthy of worship and dates back to *Bhaga*, the Vedic god who shared everything out among the adult male Aryas, including the spoils of war. He was concerned with both justice and favours, and as *Bhagavat* or *Bhagavan* became the personification of goodness and mercy. In modern India, *Bhagwan* is one of the commoner names for God and also a traditional title or mode of address for venerated scholars, saints, and gurus. Apparently, another minor Vedic god, Vishnu, fused with this deity to become one of the great gods of classical Hinduism, who also drew to himself, as avatars or incarnations, such legendary heroic figures as Narayana, Rama, and Krishna. Whatever the facts of the matter, this is the vast but beneficent personalized god who pervades the song or poem, and who provides the focus for the embroidery of further myth-making and cult-formation from the day when the *Gita* was compiled to the present moment.

The heart of the *Gita* is paradox. It teaches love in the midst of war, gentleness, detachment, and non-injury while spurring one man on to mayhem. It teaches that all is God and God is all, and yet that we are still responsible for our actions. You live, it says, in a world of distractions and illusions, and yet there is something in you that can never be distracted. *Om tat sat*—that is how it is.

The *Gita* is not a book for bleeding hearts. Arjuna is a practised warrior, but when in Chapter 11 he sees people being chomped up in the mouths of time—down to the grim detail of wee humans caught in the gaps between the great teeth—he finds the vision hard to take. The Lord's Song offers an optimistic word-picture of the cosmos at the same time as it insists on acceptance of reality in all its aspects, nice and nasty, sanctity and shit. Like a master chef, its legendary compiler, Vyasa, blends a variety of theories about that reality. One system, *Nyaya*, talks about knowledge, the knower, and what is known; it is a Hindu approach to logic and perception, and it gets its place. Another system, *Samkhya*, has a male figure called *Purusha* contrasted with a mother-nature figure called *Prakriti*; they are supposed to underlie the phenomenal world, and both are incorporated. Krishna seeks to harmonize such systems in his answer to the question with which Arjuna opens Chapter 13: effectively, what is the world?

Still other systems derived directly from the *Upanishads* and relied on the concept of Brahman underlying all things. *Vedanta* was just such a school, and is mentioned in Chapter 15. The *Gita* blends it in too and equates Brahman and Purusha as identical at the cosmic level while the *atman*—the self or soul—is identical to the *purusha* at the level of the individual. The *Gita* blends everything in a magnificent if sometimes frustrating summary of all Hindu thought up to its time, then invites us to transcend all of these systems and see something bigger that contains them all with plenty left over. Despite the chomping teeth of time and the waiting armies, it does this with grace and sympathy—none of the abstract calm of the Buddha here, nor the cold aloofness of the blank-eyed Jain saviours. They never smile, but Krishna smiles. You are not alone, the *Gita* says. You are never lost, in this world or in any world to come, Arjuna.

In expanding from the battlefield to the whole cosmos and then in shrinking back again so that Arjuna can act, the *Gita* differs radically from the Christian Gospels and from the Jewish-Christian-Muslim tradition at large. Its mouthpiece for God is not an only-begotten son or an ordained prophet—it isn't even an ascetic celibate. Krishna is an emanation, fully identified with the ultimate, one of an endless flow of such emanations or avatars. He is also a warrior prince on this occasion who, as other works make clear and everybody in India knows, had a way with the women and a zest for life. His nature and his style are quite different from Old Testament prophets such as Moses, from Jesus the carpenter of Nazareth, and from the Prophet Muhammad. The *Gita* is pantheistic, not so much in the sense that God is everything but that everything is *in* God; and pantheism, while a major theme in Hinduism, is a very minor theme indeed in the Jewish-Christian-Muslim tradition.

Even the terrifying God-vision of Chapter 11 can show only a fragment of the unguessable immensity of Vishnu. It is an immensity beyond language, and here Hinduism harmonizes with the Western religions: they all accept the ultimately indescribable quality of God. It is in the more immediate symbolism of God's relations with the world, however, that the differences are strong. In the *Gita*, for example, the divine immensity has both male and female aspects: the male germinating form, Purusha, inseminates the female reproducing form, Prakriti, and together they create all existence from their embrace.

Feminists may find the masculinity of the *Gita* and of the *Vedas* and *Upanishads* that preceded it either depressing or offensive (or both), but if they do it is worth bearing in mind this female/male dualism that is subsumed into something higher which is in ultimate terms without gender. They can also take whatever consolation they can from the throwaway lines in Chapter 9 that make liberation available *even* to women and the low-born. In the days when the *Gita* was compiled that was evidently a radical concession—a greater concession in its way than the Buddha's rather grudging willingness to allow women in as nuns into his world-renouncing Sangha or *brother*hood.

The *Gita* was conceived as a work more conservative than liberal. Its aim was to strengthen *dharma*, the social order, and to get people to perform their duties as Krishna finally persuades the reluctant Arjuna to fight, even if it means slaughtering his kin. Its radical flashes, however, have made it dear to Indian women and to other exploited groups down the centuries. After all, it tells them that if you offer Krishna a leaf, or a bowl of water, in the right spirit, then he will treat it as a princely gift. He is available to all, regardless of caste, creed, wealth, or sex, and the

Gita unequivocally says so, which may well never have been said so clearly before, anywhere.

There are people who prefer to *think* their way to salvation (whatever they understand it to be). Others prefer to *work* their way there, and others still to *feel* their way towards it, or even better into it. Most people probably waver back and forth among the three, or have a preference for one without wanting to exclude the other two. In effect, most of us operate inside a sort of triangle that is a powerful constituent both of the *Gita* and of yoga at large:

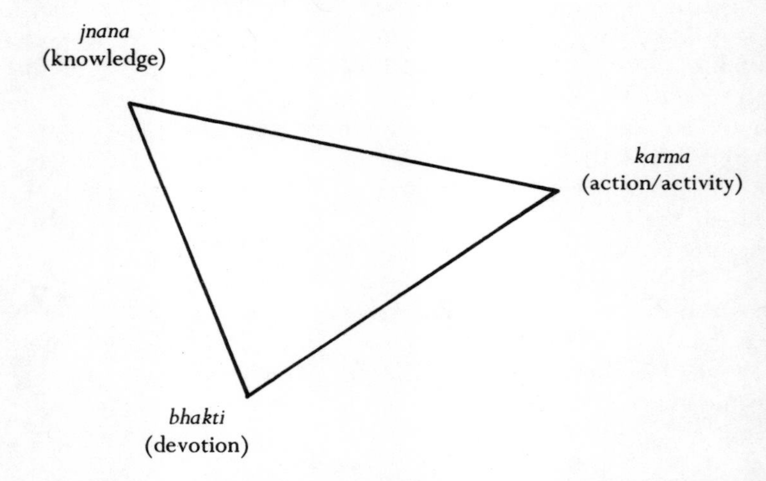

Prince Arjuna decides that he won't fight; there are too many of his kin, teachers, and friends on the enemy side. The charioteer Krishna tells him that he *must* fight; there is no going back on his duty as a kshatriya. The dialogue then moves through a variety of forms, the most important of which is a slow shift from the *jnana*, or intellectual path of the *Upanishads* (*jnana-yoga* or *jnana-marga*), using all its arguments and weighing it up along the way, through *karma*, the path of social action in which one acts for action's sake and not in any hope of reward, booty, or glory (*karma-yoga* or *karma-marga*), to *bhakti*, in which one submerges self in the greater and all-embracing Selfhood of God (*bhakti-yoga* or *bhakti-marga*).

The *Gita* moves around the triangle in the direction that is naturally most appealing to the worshippers of a god like Vishnu. It makes its own choice of the best yoga or marga, but it leaves plenty of room for the others. Someone as cerebral as Sarvepalli Radhakrishnan, the philosopher who became president of the Republic of India, could love the *Gita*, although his inclination was towards *jnana*. Someone as pragmatic as M.K. Gandhi used the *Gita* along with the Gospels as his model for non-violent political and social action—and he thought of himself as a *karma-yogi*. The triangle, it would appear, has room enough for most of us.

12.

One Hundred and Ninety-Five Threads

The *Bhagavad-Gita* and the *Yoga-sutras* of Patanjali are universally accepted as the core texts of yoga, yet when we pass from the one to the other the change in climate is profound. Where the *Gita* is a world full of life and feeling, the *Yoga-sutras* are—quite deliberately—a skeletal frame from which history and personality alike have been stripped. This work is not a song and has no wish to be poetic. It is a manual, a triumph of psychological shorthand.

A *sutra* is a thread, the word itself a distant relative of both 'sew' and 'suture'. Any brief line of thought and any collection of such aphorisms was a *sutra*, a metaphorical extension that might seem odd till one recalls that the English word 'text' belongs in the same family as 'texture' and 'textiles'.

Tradition maintains that the *Yoga-sutras* were compiled in the second century BC by the grammarian-philosopher Patanjali. This may or may not be so, but whatever the specific century or author the treatise belongs to a period when the great radical philosophies had settled down and become the domain of classifiers and systematizers. Patanjali had a particular genius for this, reducing the whole canon of 'classical' yoga to four brief books containing 195 short statements with the informative density of telegrams.

Because of this masterful conciseness, later generations have often been hard put to grasp his meaning, so that a whole industry of commentators has grown up in which sages have sought to put flesh back on Patanjali's bare bones. This proved to be a useful undertaking for two reasons quite apart from rendering a general service: it has given such commentators the opportunity to show that Patanjali shared their particular views while also adding his authority to their own. The result, however, has often been to cloud over just what the original sutras may have been all about, and has led to the introduction of later ideas and techniques which are not in fact present at all in the original. The list of commentators is long, and includes for example Vachaspati Mishra in the ninth century AD, King Bhoja in the eleventh, Madhava in the fourteenth, Ramananda in the sixteenth, Swami Vivekananda at the turn of the twentieth, and Shree Purohit Swami (with an introduction by the poet Yeats) in 1938.

Patanjali's central concern was with what he called *chitta-vritti-nirodhah*, 'the stilling of the ripples of mind-stuff'. In everyday existence our *chitta* or mind-stuff is anything but still; if it were to be stilled, however, we would encounter the *purusha* ('man' or 'person'), the true self, effectively the *atman* once again, who underlies our fevered distractions. The *vrittis* or ripples arise from experience, and may be pleasant or painful, and the only way to calm them is through detached self-control practised until it becomes habitual. The practice is ascetic but promises a great deal, insofar as it can lead to the state called *samadhi* or 'integration' (almost literally, 'getting it all together'). This state has several levels to it, dividing into an initial 'samadhi with seeds' in which personality still lingers and can result in further rebirth, and a higher 'seedless samadhi', when all the seeds of karma have been fried and the yogi is free for ever in *kaivalya*, a state of utter isolation.

Success in this inner enterprise depends on intense commitment and a devotion to 'the Lord' (*ishvara*), a special Purusha who is beyond desire, affliction, cause, and effect. This 'Lord' taught the ancient teachers and stands beyond time, but whether he is a compassionate deity like Vishnu or an impersonal exemplar like the Buddha or the Jain saviours is a matter of dispute. However, his sound-symbol is AUM, and meditation while repeating it helps one develop inner certainty in the overcoming of such obstacles as disease, lethargy, doubt, sensual pleasures, false perceptions, lack of concentration, and backsliding. Meditation, however, can proceed on any worthwhile object.

Like the Buddha, Patanjali offers the student eight steps to follow on the path. The Buddha's *arya-ashthangika-marga* or Noble Eightfold Path is almost entirely ethical: the right kind of attitude, determination, speech, behaviour, occupation, practice, awareness, and higher meditation (again *samadhi*, 'integration'), the whole leading to *nirvana* ('extinction'). Patanjali's *ashthanga-yoga* or Eight-Limb Yoga is strikingly similar and may even be in some part derivative from Buddhism, but differs in its balance of ethics and techniques. These two are probably the most famous systems of applied mysticism in the world. Both offer a commodity that must have been popular among intellectuals at the time: freedom from desire, and from the threat of being born yet again. Going to heaven (then returning again to earth) was failure—one had to eliminate every last trace of the *samskaras* or marks that life leaves upon us. Patanjali's eight steps towards this goal are:

1 YAMA ('reins'), the five major duties or great vows of self-restraint, not to be modified by time, place, purpose or even caste obligations: *ahimsa* or non-injury, a principle shared with the Buddhists and the Jains; *satya*, the truth at all times; *asteya*, refraining from theft; *brahmacharya* ('the conduct of Brahman'), chastity or celibacy in thought and action; and *aparigraha*, non-possessiveness, no interest in material things.

2 NIYAMA ('lesser reins'), the five minor duties or lesser vows: *shaucha*, inner and outer cleanliness; *santosha*, contentment; *tapas*, ascetic self-discipline; *swadhyaya*, either study of oneself or study on one's own; and *ishvara-pranidhana*, devotion to the Lord.

This ethical fundament is accepted by most yogis as the *sine qua non* of their discipline, to be established in advance of anything else. Reason enough for it lies in the stories of demon kings who acquired the powers of yoga without the responsibilities. Patanjali's system is a *sannyasa*, a regime which sets the practitioner apart from the mass of humanity in the same spirit as Buddha's order of bhikkhus and St Benedict's Rule for the monks of Western Christendom; to treat it as anything else is to distort and ultimately cheapen it. It should be no surprise that Westerners joining a yoga course and encountering something of the Eight-Limb Yoga instinctively recognize it as monastic. That is what it is. It was never designed or intended as a tool for what the Hindus call 'householders' (*grihasthas*), but for a species of recluse.

Certain powers spring from a proper application in one's life of the vows. Thus, if *ahimsa* is achieved then nobody can fight in the presence of the yogi, while if *satya* is achieved, anything that the yogi states as true becomes—instantly—true. Although the yogi rejects material things, if he attains to *asteya*, then wealth rushes at him, and if he remains truly continent in *brahmacharya*, then enormous alternative energies are tapped. Finally, when the detachment of *aparigraha* is achieved, the yogi becomes aware of what happened in his past lives.

3 ASANA ('seat'), a steady, comfortable seated position that serves to lessen one's wish to be restless and helps in transcending such opposites of life as heat and cold, pleasure and pain.

4 PRANAYAMA ('reining in the life-force'), breath-control as a systematic process of inhaling, retaining, exhaling, and restraining the breath in accordance with certain ratios, lengths of time taken and numbers of breaths in any cycle, undertaken to clarify the mind-stuff.

Nowadays, *asana* and *pranayama* are taken as the core practices of yoga courses, which in the main concentrate on manipulating the body. By now it will have become clear, however, that there is very little recorded information about physical exercises in the first thousand years or so of the subject. In particular, neither the *Gita* nor the *Yoga-sutras* says anything about 'the asanas' as opposed to 'asana'; for both Krishna's and Patanjali's *asana* is no more and no less than learning to sit still and calm the mind. The multitude of *yogasanas* post-dates both works, and belongs to two important but subsequent interrelated movements of the first millennium AD: *hatha-yoga* ('the yoga of force') and *tantra* ('the loom'). Whether Patanjali conceived of headstands and locust postures cannot be known; certainly it was left to later generations to enlarge in their own way upon the spartan foundation that he laid.

In tandem, yoga practitioners have also argued about whether exercises in breathing should be delayed until the main *yogasanas* have been mastered, presumably because Patanjali places *pranayama* after *asana*, so that it is, as it were, a later step. The only guess that seems to me possible from the data in the *Yoga-sutras* is that Patanjali advised learning to sit still before you could learn to breathe rhythmically. Again, all the edifices of asanas and pranayamas appear to have developed elsewhere, as for example in the *Hatha-yoga Pradipika* ('Light on the Yoga of Force') by Swatmarama, a much later work.

5 PRATYAHARA ('countering the senses'), sense-withdrawal, so that the mind is cut off from the normal input of life and rests in itself.

6 DHARANA ('holding'), attention or focus, so that the student develops one-pointedness (*ekagrata*) of the mind, the practice of holding the mind on one particular object or idea.

7 DHYANA ('thought'), the practice of meditation in which the mind and the object meditated upon become one; a state in which one experiences an unbroken flow of knowledge.

8 SAMADHI ('all coming together; union'), the integrated state.

Patanjali, however, discusses a special ninth condition of some importance, which he calls *samyama* ('all reined in together'). It is a blending of *dharana*, *dhyana*, and *samadhi* in terms of which he talks of 'making samyama upon' this or that. Samyama is concentration, but in such a potent form that the yogi knows and identifies with the essence of whatever he focuses upon. Out of this rise the *siddhis* or powers, as for example when the adept makes a samyama on the inner fiery breath called *udana* and can walk on water or by concentrating on *akasha* (the 'ether') can fly through the air.

However, salvation does not lie in the use of supernormal powers. The yogi who becomes too interested in them could fail to move on. If he is not careful, such powers can bear the seeds of yet another life and prevent the attainment of *kaivalya*. In Patanjali's book, omniscience might be the greatest obstacle of them all.

13. Darshana

The influence of the *Upanishads* can be seen in both the *Gita* and the *Yoga-sutras*, but the gulf between the two is nonetheless profound. The *Gita* is broad, humane and concerned; the *Yoga-sutras* are narrow, passionless, and detached. In the *Gita* an incarnate God is the prime mover and main focus; in the *Yoga-sutras* 'the Lord' is both ambiguous and a minor theme. Each work is admirably focused on its target, but it is open to question whether they are focused on the same thing and it is self-evident that they advocate different approaches to life's dilemmas.

And yet with their typical tolerant inclusiveness Hindus place these almost antithetical books side by side as the foundation texts of yoga. This can be regarded either as careless eclecticism or as yet another of those paradoxes that, with furrowed brow, we have to transcend. Or there can be a simpler way of resolving the problem, if we adopt a time-honoured Hindu means of handling such tensions. This approach probably emerged from the necessity of getting the inhabitants of such a heterogeneous land to co-exist without constant bloodshed, and it is called *darshana*.

This is yet another complex, multi-level Sanskrit word. Its basic everyday meaning is 'seeing', but by extension it can also be 'knowing', 'showing', 'teaching', and 'meeting'. In terms of a god, it is seeing and adoring; in terms of a sadhana, it is seeing and believing; in terms of a guru or in the presence of a great soul, it is seeing and benefiting simply from being there ('taking darshan', as they say). In classical terms, the *Saddarshanas* ('the Six Systems') were the great organized syntheses of the Hindu mind. Patanjali's yoga is one of them, and as such is both vision and doctrine and also—lastly and importantly—an angle of vision or special point of view.

Since the *Gita* and the *Yoga-sutras* are so palpably different but must still in some way be reconciled, it follows for Hindus that they embody two distinct but equally valid points of view. Since this world, caught in the web of maya, is a complex thing, there must be a multitude of such points of view, paths, and approaches to the same goal, along with many conceptions of that goal. Alain Daniélou regards the word *upanishad* as similar, meaning not so much a 'sitting close' to the master as a 'near approach' or approximation to the truth, to which observation he adds:

It will make us ponder over the nature of transcendent reality to discover that, according to their own logic and their means of proof, some of the 'points of view' (darśana) must be atheistic, others pantheistic, other deistic, moralistic, mystical. Yet we should not hastily conclude that these are the conflicting beliefs of philosophers. They are only the logical conclusions drawn from the premises and reached through the methods acceptable for each approach, each 'point of view'. Each one is real within its own field and aims toward the utmost limit of the reach of our faculties in a particular direction. The builders of the 'points of view' are not spoken of as thinkers or prophets but as seers (*ṛṣi*). (*Hindu Polytheism*, Pantheon, 1964)

Although these various acceptable *darshanas* or viewpoints were all within the *astika* or orthodox fold of Hinduism (because they took out the insurance of lip-service to the *Vedas* as ultimate truth), in recent centuries there has been a general tendency among thinking Hindus to see *darshanas* everywhere, including in the frameworks of such heterodox or alien systems as Buddhism, Jainism, Christianity, Islam, the Western scientific tradition, and Communism. This is a kind of cultural relativism and situational ethics prior to and complementary to modern Western anthropology, sociology, psychology, and theology. It is even foreshadowed in the *Gita*: 'Even those who follow other gods follow me, Arjuna, although not with the proper rites. I receive every sacrifice, even if the sacrificer does not know it.' (Chapter 9: see pp. 96–97).

Shri Ramakrishna in the nineteenth century was a particularly eclectic exponent of the equality of the *darshanas* (whether or not, as Krishna suggests above and as many relativists secretly believe, some *darshanas* are more equal than others). At various times he adopted the dress, lifestyle, and mentality of Christianity and Islam as well as his own multifarious religion in order the better to understand them *from within*, and afterwards taught the essential unity of all religions. His disciple Swami Vivekananda followed him in this, and also discussed this basic proposition in terms not just of different kinds of religious vision but also of different kinds of people and ways of living, using the caste system as a model for something wider:

The life of every individual, according to the Hindu scriptures, has its peculiar duties apart from what belongs in common to universal humanity. The Hindu begins life as a student, then he marries and becomes a householder, in old age he retires, and lastly he gives up the world and becomes a Sannyasin. To each of these stages of life certain duties are attached. No one of these stages is intrinsically superior to another. The life of the married man is quite as great as that of the celibate who has devoted himself to religious work. The scavenger in the street is quite as great and glorious as the king on his throne. Take him off his throne, and make him do the work of the scavenger, and see how he fares. Take up the scavenger and see how he will rule. It is useless to say that the man who lives out of the world is a greater man than he who lives in the world; it is much more difficult to live in the world and worship God than to give it up and live a free and easy life. The four stages of life in India have in later times been reduced to two—that of the householder and of the monk. (*Karma-yoga*, p. 24.)

Swami Vivekananda had himself chosen the life of the monk, and was describing the often iniquitous caste system in idealized terms strongly centred on the male, but the point comes through quite clearly nonetheless: do not assume that the *sadhana* or life-path that you are engaged on is either the only one or the best of those available, although it *may* be the right one for you. A decent *sadhana* or life-path can be built up by the determined person out of just about any set of circumstances. Anything can serve as a lever to pry yourself free: yogasanas, gymnastics, aerobics, if one wishes to work with the body; a medical career or professional soldiering, being a housewife or being an executive, being a gardener or being a clown, if it is done with right application. Athletes and artists can use their talents, while cripples can use their disabilities and arthritics their worn joints. It is, as the *Gita* might have said, all grist to Krishna's mill.

In the same book on karma-yoga, Vivekananda tells a story that highlights these points at the same time as it cuts across the inequities of the caste system and cuts through the pride of élitist yogis. It is a story designed to remind everybody that all human activities well performed have their own virtue, their own quota of power.

There was, he says, a young sannyasi who dedicated himself to a life in the forest, earnestly following the precepts of yoga and slowly acquiring merit and power. One day, however, he was meditating under a tree when some dry leaves fell on his head. He looked up and saw some birds fighting in the tree, and this made him angry.

'What is this?' he said. 'How dare you fight and drop dry leaves on my head!'

A glance was enough. A flash of fire went out from his eyes and burnt the disputatious birds to ashes. He felt rather pleased with himself; inner control was reaping external rewards, certainly enough to burn up an importunate crane and a crow. After a time, however, he grew hungry and went off to the nearby town to beg his bread, and in due course found himself before a door where he cried:

'Mother, give me food.'

A voice from inside the hut answered:

'Wait a little, my son.'

That did not please the proud young sannyasi, who thought: 'You wretched woman, making me wait like this. If you knew the kind of power I have you wouldn't do that.'

'Don't have such a high opinion of yourself, boy,' came the voice again. 'I'm not some birds fighting up in a tree.'

The sannyasi was astonished at that, and decided to wait with patience. At length the woman came out, he fell at her feet, and said: 'Mother, how did you know about that?'

'My boy,' she said, 'I do not know your yoga or your practices. I am just a common, everyday woman. I asked you to wait because my husband was ill and I was nursing him. It has been the same kind of thing all my life, a struggle to do my duty. When I was a girl I did my duty by my parents and now I do my duty by my husband—that's all the yoga I know. But by doing what I have to do I have come to see things, and so I could read your thoughts and learned what had happened in the forest. That is all I can tell you, but if you want to go higher, go to the town market. There you'll find a butcher who will tell you something you should know.'

A butcher? A killer of beasts for meat? The proud young sannyasi ate no meat, lived a chaste life and followed the rules of his order. 'Why on earth,' he asked himself, 'should I go anywhere near such a low-caste fellow?' But what he had learned had made him both cautious and curious, so he decided to do as the woman suggested.

When he reached the market he soon found the big fat butcher cutting up carcasses and talking to his customers. He was everything the sannyasi most despised. 'Probably the incarnation of a demon,' he thought, at which point the butcher looked up from what he was doing and said:

'Swamiji, did that lady send you here? Why don't you take a seat till I finish my business here?'

Shaken, the sannyasi sat down and waited, and watched, and after a time the butcher finished his work, counted his money, and said: 'Well, young sir, come with me to my home', where once again he offered him a seat and asked him to wait. The low-caste butcher then proceeded to care for his old parents, washing them, feeding them, and making them comfortable. When all this was done, he asked the young man what he could do to be of service.

The sannyasi asked to be taught higher things, and the butcher responded by giving a sermon known as the *Vyadhya-Gita*, which like the *Bhagavad-Gita* is part of the vast epic *Mahabharata*. The sannyasi was amazed by the Butcher's Song, and asked: 'How is this possible? How can you be in such a body, doing such filthy, degrading work?'

'My son,' said the butcher with a smile, 'no duty is ugly, no duty impure. My birth placed me where I am, and in my boyhood I learned my trade. I don't know your yoga, am not a sannyasi and have never retreated to the forest, but the unattached doing of my duty has had its own rewards.'

14.
The Humbling of Indra

The *Brahmavaivarta Purana* is a name to tax even the most enthusiastic Western student of Eastern mysticism, and yet it is a work that catches all the tensions and paradoxes of yogic thought in one relatively brief compass.

It is one of a collection of stories about gods and humans compiled around two thousand years ago at the most, but given the name 'The Ancient Tales' (or *Puranas*) to show that the material from which they were composed dated back into the remotest of pasts. These stories are not only remarkable for the ways in which they place the faded Vedic gods in perspective against such new super-gods as Brahma, Vishnu, and Shiva, but also for their powerful imagery, in which they came to terms with the sheer vastness of the cosmos long before modern science formulated either geological time or astronomical space. Heinrich Zimmer chose material from the *Brahmavaivarta Purana* to open his seminal work, *Myths and Symbols in Indian Art and Civilization* (1946), and I cannot conceive of a better and more truly Indian way of drawing this study to a close before I sum up in respectably logical and linear Western fashion.

Indra was king of the gods and had slain the terrible dragon Vritra, who had been holding the waters of heaven captive in his belly. He had killed the monster with his thunderbolt, releasing the imprisoned waters to the parched lands below and thus saving the world. Everybody acclaimed him, and greatly pleased with himself, Indra set about rebuilding the vast and lofty city of the gods. He felt that there had never been a hero quite as splendid as he was, and wanted a palace that would properly reflect this splendour. He therefore summoned Vishvakarman, the god of all arts and crafts, to build a palace fit for such a hero to live in.

Vishvakarman was as grateful to Indra as anyone else and undertook the task with eager enthusiasm. The result was a palace of great beauty, greater perhaps than any ever before—but Indra was never quite satisfied with it. Another tower, just one more terrace, an extra garden, some more artificial lakes; the wonders that Vishvakarman had achieved were never enough, and eventually the engineer of the gods despaired that he would ever be able to finish the work and go home. Finally, frustrated beyond endurance, Vishvakarman went beyond Indra, High King of the Gods, to seek help.

He ascended to the higher throne of Brahma the Creator, who lives far above such matters as gods, dragons, and palaces, and put his case to him. The great god Brahma was sympathetic, comforted his petitioner, and told him to descend again to the city of the gods, because soon he would be relieved of his unjust burden. Brahma then, in his turn, ascended to an even higher sphere, to the domain of Vishnu, whose agent he was. Vishnu heard him out in beatific silence, indicating simply by a nod of the head that he had understood and that all would be well.

Early the next morning a brahmin boy carrying the staff of a holy man came to the gate of Indra's palace and asked to see the king. He was hardly ten years old, but was slender and wise and drew children to him from all around. The porter felt impelled to call his master, and Indra himself came to the gate to welcome this strange but auspicious guest, inviting him into his reception hall, ceremoniously proffering him honey, milk and fruits, and at length asking him courteously why he had come.

'O King of the Gods,' said the brahmin boy, 'I heard of this mighty palace you are building, and came to ask how long Vishvakarman must labour upon it. You see, O Highest of the Gods,' and here the lad smiled a gentle, almost imperceptible smile, 'no Indra before you has ever succeeded in completing such a palace as yours is to be.'

The king was startled, and wondered if he had heard the boy correctly; then, with a fatherly smile, he said: 'Tell me, Child, are they then so very many, the Indras and Vishvakarmans you have known or at least have heard tell of?'

The strange boy nodded.

'Very many,' he said. The voice was as warm and sweet as milk fresh from the cow, but it chilled Indra none the less for that. 'Child, I knew your father Kashyapa, and your grandfather Marichi, who was the son of Brahma himself. O King of Gods, I have seen universes come and go. Who can number the passing ages or knows how often the universe has been formed again and yet again from the shapeless abyss? Who will search through the infinities of space to count the universes side by side, each with its Brahma, its Vishnu and its Shiva? And in those universes, who will count the Indras as they come and go? It may be possible to count the grains of sand and the drops of rain, but no one will ever count the number of those Indras. This is what the knowers know.'

This and more the boy said, making Indra confused and uneasy. And as he spoke, a procession of ants, well ordered like an army, in a column four yards wide, passed across the great floor of the reception hall. The brahmin boy saw them and laughed, then lapsed into a profound and thoughtful silence.

'Why do you laugh?' stammered the King of the Gods.

'I laughed because of the ants,' said the magnificent boy. 'But don't ask me to reveal their secret.'

But Indra was chastened, and begged the boy to explain the ants to him. Thus requested to teach, the boy said:

'Of those ants moving in their long parade, O King, each was once an Indra with dreams of a great palace. Each one, by virtue of pious deeds, ascended to be king of the gods, but now, through many rebirths, each has become an ant. Life is a circle, and in the cycles of time egos come and go, perishable as bubbles. Hence there is little value in attachment, and the wise are not attached to anything at all.'

At this point in the conversation an aged holy man appeared, upon whose chest was a circle of hairs, full at the outer edges but quite bare in the centre. The boy asked the holy man why this was so, and he answered:

'This circle of hairs on my chest is a source of grief to the children of the world, but even so it teaches wisdom. One hair falls with the passing of an Indra, which is why all the hairs have gone in the centre. When the rest go, then what remains of the period allotted to the present Brahma will be gone too, and I myself will die. It follows then that I am somewhat short of days. What use, therefore, is a wife or a son or a house to me? Each flicker of the eyelids of great Vishnu shows the passing of a Brahma, and everything below the sphere of a Brahma is as insubstantial as a cloud. Every joy is as flimsy as a dream, and only interferes with the one-pointedness of our attention to Vishnu alone.'

In these and in other ways the holy boy and the aged sadhu taught the chastened king, and when the lessons were ended they smiled their faint and gentle smiles—and were gone, the boy reassumed into Vishnu himself, the holy man into Shiva.

Indra was left alone in his splendid reception hall. Sadder, wiser, and somewhat afraid, he decided to leave his palace, Shachi his beautiful queen, his children, his soldiers and his servants, and seek release in a cave somewhere far away in the mountains and forests. But when she heard this, Shachi was overwhelmed with grief. In utter despair, she went to Indra's house-brahmin, the ingenious Brihaspati, and bowing at his feet begged him to intercede with her lord, to turn him away from this awful decision. Brihaspati, himself a wise magician and powerful hero in the wars against the *asuras*, listened with sympathy, comforted his royal petitioner, and taking her hand led her back into the presence of her distrait husband.

He begged a moment of the king's time, then talked wisely on the virtues first of the spiritual life and then of the secular life. He gave each its due, and spoke of how a balance must be found between them, indeed how a balance must be found in everything. He even reminded Indra and Shachi of the joys of the married state. Under the influence of his words Indra relented in his resolve to become a hermit and Shachi regained her radiant beauty—and in the meanwhile Vishvakarman had finished what he could of the palace, and gone home.

15.

Integration

Yoga is essentially applied mysticism. It takes the transcendental, even the 'supernatural', and brings them into the everyday world of schools and shops, factories and freeways, bingo and the pub. In doing this it proposes—and has proposed for at least three thousand years—that there are two orders of reality: the daily round of sights and sounds, tastes and smells, embraces, loves, hates, stupidities and laughter, and an altogether different condition that is behind, beyond, and yet somehow also *in* the daily flux.

To many people the idea of a second kind of reality is either quite out of the question (a sort of non-scientific delirium), or it is acceptable *only* in terms of the tenets, myth and symbolism of one particular religion (usually the one in which they grew up). For the mystic at large—and here I mean mystics of all nations, cultures, and backgrounds, not just yogis and swamis—the other reality is not in any way limited either by the scepticism of convinced materialists or the self-limiting metaphors of any one religion, however splendid it may appear to its believers. The second kind of reality has nothing at all to do with caste or creed, and is in itself so real to the person who has experienced it that by comparison the everyday concrete world and its religions are something close to an illusion.

If there are indeed two such orders of reality—the immediately real and the transcendentally real—then the successful mystic or yogi possesses, as it were, a double vision: of the everyday, in which x is important and y is trivial, and of the timeless, in which x is trivial and y is important. Shifts of focus across the two states of perception must be normal for such a person but rare in others, either because they are sighted for only one kind of reality, or because the other-sightedness comes only now and again, in flashes.

The best picture I can offer for this is the prism, which breaks up the oneness of light into a spectrum of colours. Someone seeing only the effects of the prism sees the many and not the one; but someone who has literally transcended the prism knows about both the broken-up light and the unbroken—or integrated—light.

As applied mysticism, yoga offers people several sets of rough options. The first of these is to take it or leave it; unlike a religion, it does not usually make any demands of adherence or membership. If it is taken up, then the next set of rough options applies: to take it seriously as a mystical discipline, or to use it as an aid to more immediate and limited ends in the everyday order of reality. Being serious will mean changing oneself in significant ways over time; being somewhat less serious and much more mundane about it can lead to all sorts of ends, some useful, some useless.

Useful ends can include using the physical techniques and advice to tone up the body and keep it fit. Here it can be an aid to the athlete or simply in the business of living. One can also use the mental exercises in order to acquire a modicum of calm and focus, as is the case for example with the techniques of Maharishi Mahesh Yogi's Transcendental Meditation movement.

Useless ends can include various kinds of self-deception: a dilettante dabbling in the mysterious, offering a sort of escape from one's basic problems into woolly-minded occultism and alternative metaphors about life to those in which one grew up.

If one is serious, however, a final set of rough options opens up:

1. To distance oneself physically and/or psychologically from the everyday world, first through a special act of renunciation (*sannyasa*), then through a clearly delineated daily discipline (*sadhana*), becoming at one end of the spectrum an ascetic recluse, or at the other a member of an order that is in the world but not of it. In adopting this role, yoga *sannyasis* are not unlike Buddhist or Christian monks, and for them the primary rule could very well be the *Yoga-sutras* of Patanjali.

2. To remain physically and psychologically involved with the world, and to participate in its business (which could include its sexuality, its styles of diet, even its warfare if the cause was just, but could also mean [a degree of] celibacy, vegetarianism, and pacifism, depending on the personality and goals of the individual concerned). By engaging in everyday family and career but at the same time developing one's awareness of the other reality, such a person places the transient daily round in a new perspective. In such circumstances, the yogi is active in the world while also inactive in it, attached and yet detached, and a basic guide for such a lifestyle could be the *Bhagavad-Gita*.

An infinity of personal variations is possible, and to highlight how these variations fit into the dynamic of the modern yoga movement I would like to resurrect the Yoga Box, a device I described in the *SYA Journal* of July 1979. The box is simply an aid and should not be taken too seriously. Everybody involved in yoga seems to me to occupy a position somewhere in the box, and may as the years pass move around within it. I have numbered the points in the box 1, 2, 3, 4 and 5 for convenience and labelled them in terms of the continuums or spectrums that seem to me to dominate the movement today:

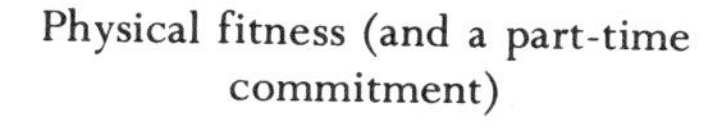

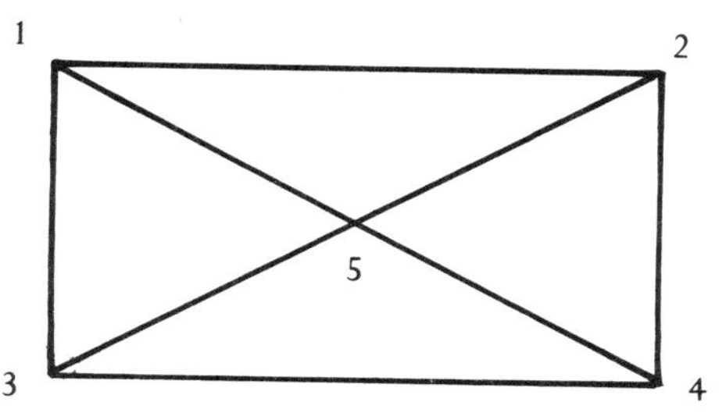

Most people who attend yoga courses start off in Corner 1, and either stay there, go away completely, or begin to move further into the box. Most people and movements operate along a line or within triangles. The Friends of Yoga, for example, as developed by Wilfred Clark, seem to me to operate along Line 2–3, with occasional sallies towards (but not into) Corner 4. The practitioners of 'Iyengar yoga' to my mind operate along Line 1–4, with inclinations towards Corner 2, although they might see themselves as operating inside the whole Triangle 1–2–4. Certain quasi-religious groups like the Raja-yogis of Mount Abu and the Ramakrishna Mission operate inside Triangle 2–3–4, but usually well towards Line 2–4. But I must confess the place that has always intrigued me in this picture is Point 5, where everything meets in dynamic equilibrium.

The cross-over point in someone's life-path, from a general interest in something like yoga to a strong and steady commitment, is not necessarily sudden, spectacular, or even conscious (although it could be any or all of these things). It could be a vague, creeping experience over years, only identifiable in retrospect—well after the unnoticed divide had been crossed. The goal, however, is identifiable enough, and well described by the word 'integration', a Western word that conveys much of what 'yoga' conveys in Hindu terms.

Integration is 'unification into a whole' (*Chambers Twentieth Century Dictionary*, 1983) or 'the co-ordination of mental processes into an effective personality' (*Longman Dictionary of the English Language*, 1984). This is presumably what the yogi means by being yoked or unified. It is a rare state, but one towards which people—aware of their inner confusions and inconsistencies—constantly yearn; long before the Californian cultural revolution, people have wanted to get their heads and their acts together and make love, not war. Indeed, the drive to become a whole person and to see the world whole may be a basic evolutionary imperative in our species.

Several students of mysticism, religion, and life have suggested this, among them Shri Aurobindo in Pondicherry and Swami Vishnudevananda in Rishikesh and Montreal. This is the belief that lies behind those movements which like to think in terms of a new 'Aquarian' age, of the human becoming divine, and of Man being permanently aware of God. Strict rationalists always feel uncomfortable with such movements and with slogans like Cosmic Consciousness, but they also—more than most—believe in evolutionary progress, which implicitly contains the idea that the 'human' is an intermediate condition between 'animal' and 'god'. The process of evolution has been described since the time of Darwin himself as an 'upward' line out of the mindless primeval ooze and into an increasingly humane higher consciousness, whether deity as such exists or not.

Abraham Maslow, one of the founders of the movement called 'humanistic psychology', saw the phenomena of mysticism, yoga, and religion as lying squarely in the area of rational scientific inquiry. In the course of his investigations, he formulated a simple, five-point scale of human needs, arguing that when each 'lower' need is sufficiently satisfied, then the next and 'higher' need emerges and takes charge of the human organism. In their rising sequence, the five needs are:

1. for food, drink and exercise (the physiological level)
2. for shelter, security and order (the safety level)
3. for belonging, love and acceptance (the social level)
4. for acknowledgement, status and prestige (the esteem level)
5. for fulfilment and growth (the level of self-actualization)

Maslow saw these needs as all simultaneously present but latent in every human being. Circumstances can just as easily cause someone to revert to a lower level of need as to ascend to a higher level. The fifth level can, in Maslow's view, lead to 'peak experiences' of a mystical nature, variously experienced by different people according to their expectations and their environments, and allows for a state in which such awareness becomes less a matter of isolated occasional *peaks* and more a matter of a steady *plateau* effect:

Plateau-experiencing can be achieved, learned, earned by long, hard work. It can be meaningfully aspired to. But I don't know of any way of bypassing the necessary maturing, experiencing, living, learning. All of this takes time. A transient glimpse is certainly possible in the peak-experiences which may, after all, come sometimes to anyone. But, so to speak, to take up residence on the high plateau of Unitive consciousness—that is another matter altogether. That tends to be a lifelong effort. It should not be confused with the Thursday evening turn-on that many youngsters think of as *the* path to transcendence. For that matter, it should not be confused with *any* single experience. The 'spiritual disciplines', both the classical ones and the new ones that keep on being discovered these days, all take time, work, discipline, study, commitment . . . Man has a higher and transcendent nature, and this is part of his essence, i.e., his biological nature as a member of a species which has evolved.' (Abraham Maslow, *Religions, Values and Peak-Experiences,* Viking, 1970, pp. xv–vi.)

This kind of statement is less unusual now in the West than it would have been before the Second World War, when only a few thinkers like Teilhard de Chardin linked mystical experience with biological theories of evolution. Nowadays, students of mystical techniques quite routinely discuss the possibility, and also from research and observation across the world draw maps of what Maslow's plateau of the spirit might be like. W. T. Stace, for example, has created a typology or list of the nine features that are common to all mystical traditions. These are so universally reported upon that they present a strong prima-facie case for accepting that such phenomena exist—as valid non-neurotic, non-psychotic experiences demanding the serious attention of psychologists, anthropologists, sociologists, and others who assert that they are scientists interested in understanding reality. Stace's nine features are:

1. a sense of the unity of self and universe, in which the ego fades into a state of 'pure awareness'
2. a sense of transcending both time and place
3. a sense of bliss and peace
4. a sense of the numinous
5. a conviction of the reality (that is, the non-hallucinatory nature) of the experience, both at the time and afterwards
6. a resolution of the paradoxes or oppositions of life, such as moving and yet being at rest
7. a conviction of the ineffability of the experience; it cannot be put into words

8. an awareness of its transience; it cannot be indefinitely sustained
9. subsequent changes in attitude and behaviour; one is not the same afterwards, but is marked by a new and intuitive kind of knowledge

It is unfortunately the case that anybody who has not had the experience cannot know for sure whether it exists or not, or how it 'feels'. Partial experience, however, suggests for many that fuller experiences exist, and in many traditions the assurance by certain 'masters' that they have had the beatific vision for longer or shorter periods is enough for most aspirants.

It is my own view, both as a student of language and of yoga, that language cannot be expected to convey the kind of holistic communion described by mystics, because language is by its nature atomistic and linear: it operates in bits and pieces called words and sentences, needs a span of time in order to be effective, and comes out in thin strips, as it were. It is not large enough for the job, but it is the best we have and can be made to do quite a lot if we do not expect it to do everything.

Even strict, logical language can achieve a great deal in helping unravel the mysteries of existence, as both the Hindu sutras and Western science demonstrate. The closer, however, one goes to the second order of reality, the less successful strict rationalism is, and the more useful myth and fantasy language. This is why the rishis and the saints have always tended to talk in parables, and why I have set half at least of this book in story form. A 'parable' is parabolic, and comes at the truth from unexpected angles, taking both it and the reader by surprise. By its riddle-like qualities it forces the mind-brain into a new mode of thought, demands participation, and may like a Zen *koan* provide the necessary flash of understanding in which the reader or listener for the first time 'sees' what is meant.

Among the greatest parables that our species has produced is the account of Krishna the charioteer and Arjuna the royal bowman, in the *Bhagavad-Gita*. Take the story literally, and you can enjoy a fable from a vanished age. Take it figuratively—parabolically—and it kneads the mind like dough. If words cannot describe the indescribable, and they cannot, then the *Gita* like everything else is a failure, but in the best spirit of yoga, it can succeed while it fails.

PART TWO

THE GUIDE TO INTEGRATION

The Bhagavad-Gita

Lead-in

The *Gita* is a conversation—however one-sided—between two warriors of ancient India. One is Arjuna the son of Pandu, a fair-skinned Aryan prince, the other the dark-skinned Krishna, leader of the Vrishni clan and a god walking among men.

The setting for the conversation is a chariot, just before the battle for the kingdom of Hastinapura, between the sons of Pandu and their kinsmen the Kauravas. Krishna is the charioteer and Arjuna the royal archer whose duty it is to sow death among those relatives and friends whom fate has put on the enemy side.

The subject of the conversation is therefore duty, life and death, and the nature of reality. The obvious question is whether Arjuna should fight or not. The less obvious and much larger question is whether each individual human being, faced with the world, its obligations, its joys and its horrors, should accept that world and act in it, or reject it and seek a private salvation.

1 THE BATTLEFIELD

What happened on the field of Kurukshetra? What happened when the two armies met?

The Kauravas and the Pandavas now faced each other, and the numbers were great on both sides. They were led by famous princes and fierce captains, hordes of men drawn up and ready to fight for the kingdom. War-drums rattled and horns sounded; the war-cries and blaring conch-shells were terrible to hear. There would soon be flights of arrows, and the battle would begin.

Prince Arjuna, son of Pandu, was a formidable soldier. He sat in his chariot, and Krishna, the leader of the Vrishnis, held the reins of the white horses for him. When Arjuna gave the command the charioteer urged the beasts forward, so that the great chariot in all its martial splendour left the Pandava lines, and went out into the space between the armies. There Arjuna could survey the enemy more clearly.

But there was no pleasure in it. He saw only kinsmen, erstwhile friends and teachers, all drawn up against him and against his brothers. It felt ominous. He had no wish to kill those people, although he was a soldier—a kshatriya—by caste. He had no wish to gain anything—even a kingdom—through their deaths. Such killing would be the end of proud families, would be the breaking of ancient laws of kinship.

'Women will be raped and castes defiled,' he said to his charioteer. 'Don't the men who cause such things go down to hell? I would rather die, myself, than cause such bloody confusion. I'd rather lay my weapons down, here and now, and just wait to be killed.'

And, quite out of keeping with his proud fierce reputation, the prince let go of his bow and arrows, and sank down in despair.

2 THE DEATHLESS SELF

His charioteer turned to him, surprised by such despairing words, and answered him sharply:

'Remember who you are, Arjuna! You can't behave in such an un-Aryan way as that, like some low and snivelling eunuch! Come, burner of your enemies, stand up and fight.'

'I would rather eat beggars' food than kill my sacred teacher Drona and those others,' said the prince. 'You can advise me—but I will not fight.'

Krishna smiled at that—and there, in that place between two armies, he began to talk.

'There is no point in worrying about the fate of these men,' he said. 'Woven into the whole of this visible world is something that never dies. There never was a time when I didn't exist, or you or any of these warriors—and there never will be such a time. Bodies come and go, but this eternal something never changes, though it is there in every body. It doesn't kill and it isn't killed. It was never born and will never die, and nothing happens to it when the body is killed. You know how easily a man changes his clothes; in the same way this inner something casts off its old worn body and takes on a new one. No weapon or fire can hurt it, you know; water can't wet it or the winds dry it out. It is deathless and changeless. It lies beyond all such cutting and burning and wetting and drying.

'Everything that is born has to die, and everything that dies has to be born again. But there's no need to grieve over it! That is how things are.

'So remember your warrior's duty. Is there anything better for a kshatriya than a just war? If you don't fight, do you expect people to go on honouring you? The chariot troops will think you are some sort of coward, and they'll forget all your earlier triumphs, and start saying things about you that you can hardly want them to say. But if you fight, what is the problem? If you are killed, there's a warrior's heaven to go to—if you live, there's a fine kingdom to inherit. So fight!

'Isn't detached duty your business? Forget everything else—the quibblings of brahmins, your thoughts of reward. Rise above all that. Treat success and failure as the same. With a disciplined mind you can do it, and can even free yourself from birth and death. Your consciousness can reach beyond illusion, beyond all past and future scriptures, beyond such contradictions as there are on earth, to find an unshaken state, the yoga of steady wisdom.'

'What is a man like in such a state?' asked Arjuna. 'What on earth does he do with himself? How does he speak or sit or walk, this man?'

'He has given up all desires and pleasures,' said Krishna. 'He is aware of his inmost self, the atman. A man like that is steady and wise, not buffeted by grief or flooded out with joy. He is beyond passion and the emotions, beyond even love and hate. Like a tortoise he pulls in his senses. The impressions of the world might still tear at him, but he will sit there, harnessed, controlling his senses—intent on the ultimate. If a man gives way to the senses, their power will grow, and he will become confused and forget his duty. It's the end if that happens. But it doesn't happen to the disciplined man; he can move through the whole world undisturbed. The man with an unharnessed mind has no wisdom, no peace, no achievement. He is blown like a little boat before the wind. His brightest noontime is midnight to the sage. Waters flow into an ocean and the ocean can always take a little more. It's the same with a wise man; he can absorb his pleasures in peace. He does not say "This is me" or "This is mine". His is the fixed still state of brahman, beyond perplexity, and in that state at his time of death he goes forward into nirvana.'

3 THE YOGA OF ACTION

Krishna's words served only to bewilder Arjuna, and he said:

'If you think that going off into some kind of transcendental state is so much better than action, then why prod me into this cruel fight? You are muddling me. Advise me more simply than this.'

'It's a long time,' said Krishna, 'since I first proposed two laws, one for the contemplative man and one for the man of action like you. The first is jnana-yoga, and the second is karma-yoga. But don't suppose that even someone who chooses to sit still and renounce the world can escape from action, from karma. There are twining strands in nature, and they force action on everybody. Someone who disciplines his limbs and withdraws from activity hasn't forgotten about it, although he might hypocritically persuade himself that he has. No. More effective is the man who reins in his senses, then goes about his work with detachment, a karma-yogi. Action is better than attempts at inaction. So do what you have to do! If you don't do things, you won't even manage to keep yourself fit. The world is a welter of activity, but a certain kind of action, the kind that is offered up like a sacrifice, can free you from attachment, from the bonds of desire and pleasure.'

He talked then about many other things. Among them was Prajapati, the creator. In creating the world he sacrificed himself for it—and called on men to do the same. That spirit of sacrifice was like a wonderful cow, he said, that gives you all the milk you could ever want. The Vedas taught that everything depends on sacrifice, men helping the gods and then gods helping men. Only a selfish man would opt out of such a partnership, cooking food only for himself, never offering up any of it. Food is the foundation of life, and needs rain to nourish it. The rain in turn is sent by the gods, appeased with sacrifice. That was the turning of the wheel, and it was an evil man who would not try to help it in its turning.

'Only in the atman is real satisfaction to be found,' said Krishna. 'Someone who appreciates this is detached when he does his duty, is beyond such things as activity and inactivity. King Janaka was like that, when he achieved perfection. The world needs such examples to follow. Think of me. I have all I want and don't need to do anything anywhere in the three worlds—but I'm not idle. If I did nothing, wouldn't men imitate me and give up their work too? That wouldn't do the world any good, would it?

'The ignorant,' he said, 'are snared in their doings, but a wise man isn't snared at all. Of course, he won't go about telling the ignorant how unenlightened they are. Harnessed in his discipline, he goes about his work, and lets other people do what they want to do. The twining strands of nature make karma—whatever an egotist may care to think of his own important doings. The wise man knows this and stands back, watching nature's strands twining, snaring, deceiving. He sees things whole, where others only see bits and pieces. So concentrate on the ultimate self, forget your ego and the urge to possess and get involved. Cast off this besetting fever and fight!

'You must act, you know—but you shouldn't be snared in the passions and hatreds of life. They wait like robbers in ambush for you. You mustn't sidestep your duty, because it is *yours*, and however badly you do it it's better than doing some other fellow's duty well. It's better to die following your own dharma than embarking on someone else's.'

'Why then do men do evil, pushed into it against their better intentions?' asked Arjuna.

'Greed pushes them. Anger pushes them. Passion pushes them. These are the true enemies, and they help the poor ego to masquerade as the inmost self, the atman. As smoke clouds the purity of fire—as grime obscures the brightness of the mirror—as an embryo is wrapped darkly in its womb, so the truth is easily concealed by such illusions. Wisdom is snared among the flames of a shape-shifting lust that can never be satisfied. It lurks everywhere—around your senses, in the mind, and even in the higher consciousness, buddhi itself. It smothers wisdom. So, my bold stallion, you must curb the senses first and destroy this destroyer of knowledge, whether sacred or profane. The senses are great, so they say, and the mind is greater still. Greater still than that is buddhi, the seat of reason—but beyond lies the atman. Aware of that ultimate self, be steady and at peace. And strike the enemy, however elusive he may be.'

4 THE YOGA OF KNOWLEDGE

'Once, a long time ago, I explained all this to Vivasvat, the sun. He told it to Manu, the first man, and Manu passed it on to Ikshvaku. So the tradition was handed down, and the royal seers learned it, the kingly rishis. But in course of time the yoga was lost. It is a great mystery, this ancient lore, and I am only telling it to you now because you are my loyal friend.'

Arjuna was wretched and bewildered. He said: 'You were born *later* than the sun. The sun was created long *before* you. What on earth do you mean by saying such things as "I explained this yoga long ago"?'

'Arjuna, I have had many births, and so have you—but I remember all of mine, and you remember none of yours. In my ultimate self though, I am changeless and am never ever born at all. I am the lord of all beings, and through my power of maya I blend with nature and take shape. Whenever the rightful dharma fails and anarchy appears, then I project myself in a form like this. I reappear from age to age, for the protection of the good and the destruction of evil-doers, and to rebuild the social order. Anyone who comprehends that truth, Arjuna, escapes rebirth. Many folk—their passions, fears and angers spent—purified in the burning force of enlightenment, have learned this and been absorbed into me. Others, however, look only for material rewards in this world, and in sacrificing to its gods attain a more limited prize.

'I created the four great castes, each according to its nature. I did that, but you must also understand that I have never ever done anything at all. Karma doesn't bind me, nor do I yearn for any reward, and if you can come to terms with that you too won't be bound by karma. The ancients realized this and so can you. It is the answer to a question that bewilders even the sages: What is action and its opposite, inaction? The man who can see inaction in the midst of acts, and actions where all else is inactive—he is really a yoked one, and wise. His karma is burned up in the fire of enlightenment. A man like that does nothing even when he seems most active. He has passed beyond the dualities of pleasure and pain, beyond jealousies, beyond success and failure. He is unbound—dissolved.

'Yogis offer up their sacrifices in many ways: Some offer to the gods, while others restrain their senses, practise severe austerities, undertake the control of the breath and of diet. All of these are a means of attaining the eternal brahman.

'You are puzzled now—but when you begin to appreciate that all things are there within you, in your own deepest self, and that in turn the self exists in me, then you will no longer be puzzled. Even if you were the worst of evil-doers, you could escape the waters of evil in the boat of that enlightenment. A fire burns things to ashes, and in just that way does jnana burn karma to ashes.

'A man with the necessary faith, and with his senses curbed, gains enlightenment, but an ignorant faithless doubting fellow certainly doesn't. For him there will be no such happiness. So, with the sword of enlightenment cut out all these ignorant doubts lurking in your heart, adopt this yoga—and *stand up,* proud warrior!'

5 THE YOGA OF RENUNCIATION

Arjuna said: 'This is all very well, Krishna. First you tell me to renounce all action, then you bid me get to work. Be clear—which is the better of these two?'

'Both can take you to the highest goal. But consider the man who renounces action. He has no hates or cravings, and stands beyond the contradictions of life. Such a yogi is undefiled, and attains brahman swiftly. While seeing and hearing, touching and smelling, eating and walking and sleeping and breathing and talking and defecating and the like—even in blinking his eyes!—he remembers that his bodily minions are at their tasks, not his essential self. Nothing stains him, any more than a lotus petal is stained by the water in which it lies.

'The self sits within the body, the city of the nine gates, neither acting nor compelling action in others, and as it sits there nature toils away.

'These enlightened ones, they see the same essence in a wise and courtly brahmin, in a cow, in an elephant, in a dog or in an outcaste. Though still in this world, they have eluded its snares. They are shaken neither by gain nor by loss, which go together and have no permanence. The yogi has a joy and a light inside him, attaining union with brahman while alive, and going on at death to the nirvana that is also brahman. The silent sage, the muni, shuts out all external things, fixing his gaze between the brows, making the incoming and outgoing breaths even in the nostrils, his senses and mind and higher consciousness all in check—and he is free. In knowing me he finds peace, and this is all very good indeed.'

6 THE NATURE OF YOGA

'But there is a kind of man who renounces the world and yet works on in it. He is a sannyasi, a yogi. He uses karma to reach the heights, and after that he is at peace.

'A man should rise up, not sink down. His self can be a friend, but it can also be an enemy. There are, you see, two selves—higher and lower. Don't let the carnal self sink down. Raise it by means of the higher innermost self. When that self is absorbed in inner joy, it is at peace, disregarding such contrasts as heat and cold, pleasure and pain, honour and disgrace. Someone in that state is a yogi, and gold and dirt are the same to him. He can even look on friends and on enemies with detachment.

'Alone in a secluded place the yogi puts himself in harness, controlling the mind, having no hopes and possessing nothing. He takes up a steady seat in a clean place, not too high or too low, with a cloth or a hide or some grasses on it. There he sits and makes his mind one-pointed, restraining his thoughts and senses. Quite still—his body, neck and head all in an upright line—he fixes his gaze on the tip of his nose. He sits—stilled, fearless, continent, controlled, harnessed, intent on me. A yogi like that reaches the peace of my nirvana.

'Arjuna, this yoga is not for someone who eats too much or doesn't eat at all, for someone who sleeps too much or doesn't sleep at all. It is for the person who knows a middle way in eating and in resting, in expressions and in actions, in sleeping and in waking—and this yoga destroys all pain. When thought is checked and is stilled in the self alone, then a man escapes desire and we call him yukta—the yoked one, the unified one. The yogis who control their thoughts and discipline themselves in this way are like a lamp that stands quite steady in a windless place. In stillness they achieve the joy of self-awareness, and—for so they think—in this stillness they achieve a prize beyond all others. They have uncoupled the link with earthly suffering, have withdrawn themselves, and resist the fickle straying of the mind. They see the self in all things, see that all things are the same, see me in everything and everything in me. Such men are said to be the highest of all yogis.'

'But my mind is restless, Krishna!' said Arjuna. 'I can't imagine this still and balanced state. The mind is as hard to curb as the very wind.'

'That is true, but it can be done.'

'But, strong-armed Krishna, suppose a man believes this, but while believing it he tries and fails. What then? Is he lost, vanishing like a scattered cloud?'

'No, he isn't lost, not in this world or any world to come. He will get a reward of years in heaven, and in the proper course of time will be born again in a good house. He might even be born into a family of yogis, which is quite a privilege. In that new life he carries on the struggle, rising above the wordy Vedas, and through many lifetimes he strives until at last he gets there. A yogi like that is more than just an ascetic, more than a mere speculator or a ritualist. Be a yogi like that, Arjuna, and be committed to me.'

7 THE NATURE OF KRISHNA

'Fix your mind on me, Arjuna, practise this yoga, and trust me. Listen, and you'll start to realize just what I am.

'Of all the endless thousands of men, only one here and there seeks enlightenment, and among those few there are even fewer who know me as I really am.

'I am nature as you perceive it to be, and in that form I have eight parts: I am earth and water, fire and air, and the void too; I am mind and I am consciousness and I am even the ego. But, strong-armed warrior, I have another nature too, beyond that, and it is that other nature that generates all living things, and then sustains them. Every living being depends on both these natures, for the universe has its start and finish in me. There is nothing higher, and all creation is strung out on me like beads on a thread.

'I am the taste in water, the light in the sun and the moon. I am the syllable Aum in the Vedas, the sound in the void and the manhood in men. I am the scent in the earth and the spark in the fire. I am the life in all creatures, the energy that burns in the effort of ascetics. I am the very first of all seeds, Arjuna, the light in the mind and the brilliant sharpness of the flame. I am strength in the strong—but I experience no wrongful lust, no passion that conflicts with dharma.

'There are three states in nature, three strands, three gunas—and they come from me. They are the virtuous sattva, the passionate rajas and the dark and heavy tamas. They are in me, but I am not in them. They serve to snare and delude the whole world, which can't perceive that I lie beyond them, unchanging and undying. Out of these gunas is woven my maya, a power that is hard to escape. Only those that trust me can get beyond *that* uncanny force.

'Evil-doers don't put their trust in me and so maya deludes them, and they follow the ways of the anti-gods. Good folk exist in many kinds, some suffering, some seeking rewards for what they do, others seeking wisdom. The best of them is the seeker of wisdom, the jnani, the yukta. I am dear to him and he is dear to me—but a man like that, at the apex of many lifetimes of effort, is hard to find.

'It is the common way of men to chase their lusts, to trust to all sorts of gods, to follow all sorts of rules and paths. That is how it is. I sanction it, and will indeed strengthen a man's faith in his god, so that he can get his heart's desire. Such gods, however, lead no farther than themselves. They are finite, and I am not. The unenlightened, of course, see me here as just another short-lived man. Because of the web of maya they can't see my real unchanging state. I know them and every creature that has ever been or is or ever will be, but none of them know me. Men are confused by dualities, by contradictions arising out of their greed and hate. A few escape the dualities and revere me. They seek release from age and death, and they will come to know brahman and atman and the nature of karma. They will understand both my natures, and with unified understanding they will know me when they die.'

8 THE NATURE OF BRAHMAN

'What is this brahman?' asked Arjuna. 'And what is atman, and what is karma, best of all men? Tell me. What is it that shapes the ways of mortals and of gods? And how, at the time of death, does a yogi know you?'

'Brahman is universal and beyond destruction, but when found within you is called atman, the self. Karma is the very force of creation that brings all the different beings into existence.

'Anyone who thinks of me when he is dying enters into my very nature. You see, a man's state of mind at time of death shapes his future. You should therefore think of me always, remembering me as you fight. I am the sun that shines on the other side of darkness. One who closes all the gates of the body, and, keeping a steady mind, centres the energy of life—the prana—between his brows, goes to the supreme one. He utters the timeless syllable Aum and goes out on the highest path, finding me easily enough, and in me the highest prize.

'All the worlds pass away, Arjuna, even the world of Brahma, but such a man as that is born no more into them. A single day of Brahma lasts a thousand ages, and a night of Brahma is just the same. At the dawning of such a day the different forms spring from the one, the seen from the unseen, and they all dissolve again when great night falls. That is the cycle of things, going and coming without volition. Beyond all that, beyond both the seen and the unseen, is a high and primal state, and those who go to him never return. Bhakti reaches him—loyalty and love. On him all things hang, the spinner of all the worlds.'

9 THE ROYAL MYSTERY

'Let me tell you something very strange, but very real,' said the blessed one. 'I'll tell it to you because you aren't obstinately contesting what I say. If you accept it, you will escape from the ills of rebirth. It is the ageless and mysterious wisdom of the kings, who learned it through direct experience. It isn't hard to practise, and is in harmony with dharma, the law. Men who don't appreciate it are bound forever on the wheel.

'I am that unseen spinner of all the worlds. All beings depend on me, but I do not depend on them. I transcend them—I sustain them—but I do not depend on them for anything. Like a great wind blowing where it will through boundless space, so all beings depend on me. When a world-age ends all creatures are drawn back into my nature, my prakriti. When a new age dawns I radiate them out again. So through this prakriti I send out again and again the host of helpless forms. But such actions don't bind me, Arjuna my winner of loot. Instead, I sit among them all, detached from them all. I look on, and my prakriti brings forth all that moves and all that stays still, and the wheel of the world turns.

'There are fools who spurn me here and now in this human form; they can't see that I am lord of all. Their hopes, their actions and their beliefs are all in vain, and in delusion they embrace a dark and devil-ridden prakriti. Some, however, know me. These great ones revere me and keep their vows. They are the yuktas. And there are others who sacrifice to me as the one who is also many. I am the rite and the sacrifice and the offering for the dead and the healing herb and the sacred mantra and the ghee and the fire and the oblation placed in the fire. I am the father and the mother of this world and all else besides; I am Aum and the three Vedas. I am the way and the witness, the sustainer, the beginning, the middle and the end, the seed that never changes. I am the one who gives out heat and holds back the rain or lets it fall. I am both immortality and death, both what is and what is not.

'There are men who know the Vedas, who drink the soma juice and are free of defilement. They go to Indra's heaven and enjoy there the pleasures of the gods. But when they have enjoyed that expansive paradise in full, their merit exhausted, they return to this world of mortal men. Even those great pleasures pass. But to the people who revere and meditate on me—and persevere in it—I give a fuller liberation.

'Even those who follow other gods follow me, Arjuna, although not with the proper rites. I receive every sacrifice, even if the sacrificer doesn't know it. But to the gods go the worshippers of the gods, to their ancestors go the ancestor-worshippers, and to ghosts go the worshippers of ghosts.

'Those that worship me, however, come to me.

'Whoever offers me no more than a leaf or a flower or a fruit or some water, if it is given with love and a pure heart, I accept it. So whatever you do or eat or offer in sacrifice or give away in alms, offer it to me; and whatever harsh austerity you may perform, son of Queen Pritha, do it for me. This will break the bonds of karma, whose fruits are so mixed, and with the steady detachment of yoga you will win to me.

'I am the same to all beings. I hate none and favour none, but those who come close to me in bhakti abide in me and I in them. However evil a man's way of life, if he worships me without distraction, in love, he will swiftly change and attain peace. Arjuna, someone who loves me is never lost.

'Son of Queen Pritha, those who seek refuge in me will find it, whether they are of low birth or women or traders or serfs on a farm. How much more then the holy brahmins and the royal sages who take up bhakti? You are in an ever-changing and grievous world, so love and worship me. Fix your mind on me, your goal, and you will find me.'

10 ARJUNA'S PLEA

'My strong-armed friend,' said Krishna, 'no one knows where I come from, not the gods or the rishis, for they are all come out of me. All the states of mortal men come out of me, whether it's their intelligence or sense of truth, their joy and sorrow, their being or not being, their fear or their freedom from it, their honour or their disgrace. The seven ancient rishis and the four Manus came from my mind, and from them came all mortal men. I am the source of all, and out of compassion I dispel the murk of ignorance with my lamp.'

'You are the supreme brahman,' said Arjuna, 'the highest home, the highest vessel of purity, primordial god, the purusha, unborn and all-pervading. The sages such as Narada and Vyasa told us this, and now you tell us yourself. I believe, Krishna, knowing that neither gods nor anti-gods appreciate that all this world bursts forth from you. Tell me more! Tell me how to know you and in what forms to think of you when I meditate. I can't have enough of your deathless words.'

'Listen then, and I will tell you some of my forms, the most important anyway—for to my forms there is no limit. I am the atman deep in your being; I am its beginning, middle and end. Among the gods of the sky I am Vishnu, both the sun and the moon. Among the gods at large I am Indra, and among the gods of storms I am Shiva. In the netherworld they call me Kuvera. Of the great household priests I am Brihaspati, among warlords Skanda, among seers Bhrigu, and among utterances I am Aum. In all groupings I am the foremost.

'Among the Vrishnis I am called Krishna, but among the sons of Pandu I am Arjuna. I am the rod of the powerful, the silence in mysteries and the wisdom of the wise. I am the seed of all things, and there is no limit to my powers, Arjuna burner of enemies. But what I have just said is only a part. Whatever exists and has beauty, it arises from just one fragment of my beauty. Unchanging, I support.'

11 THE UNIVERSAL VISION

'In your compassion,' said Arjuna, 'you have explained to me your Self, the greatest of all mysteries. My bewilderment has gone. Lotus-eyed Krishna, you have described to me the ebb and flow of life, and your own unchanging glory. I accept it—but what is it like? If you think I can stand it, lord of yoga, show me this unchanging self.'

'All right,' said Krishna. 'You will see my forms in their hundreds of thousands, in all their shapes and shades. You will see the parade of all the gods, all the universe centred in One, everything that moves and everything that is still, all within my body. But mortal eyes won't do for a vision like that. I must give you a higher kind of sight, and then you will really see.'

And, having said this, Krishna, the great lord of yoga, appeared to the prince in his ultimate guise. If a thousand suns rose all together it might have been a little like what Arjuna saw. He was stricken by it. His hair stood on end, and he bowed his head and joined his hands and said:

'Oh God, in your body I see gods! I see all the host of life too. I see Brahma the lord of creation on his lotus throne, with all the demi-gods and ancient rishis. Everywhere there are countless arms and bellies and mouths and eyes—no beginning to them, no midpoint to them, no end to them, all in a single shape that is every shape. It is an infinite beauty—in it I see you, and yet in that brilliance you are hard to see. Now I understand how you can be deathless, the fundament of everything, the primal being.

'Your arms are beyond counting. Your mouth is a furnace burning up the very universe! You spread between the heights and the depths and make whole worlds shudder. Hosts of gods pour into you as I look, their hands pressed together. Everyone worships you—gods, saints, ancestors and anti-gods alike. The worlds shake in seeing your size, your mouths, your limbs, your bellies, your fearful teeth. If they do that, how much more should *I* tremble?

'You blaze—You touch the sky—Your mouths yawn—Your eyes distend. I can't stand it! Your mouths are like burning time, jagged with clashing teeth. I am lost! Have mercy!

'But who are these? Are they the armies drawn up here, the Kauravas, sons of Dhritarashtra, my teacher Drona and the rest? They charge headlong and blind into your jaws, crushed there, some caught in the gaps between your teeth, heads chomped to powder. All those heroes, borne in a swelling tide into those burning mouths! Moths go to the flame, and like them whole worlds charge and jostle crazily into your maw. You lick them up—burning, eating, eating them all. Vishnu! Your scorching beams fill the universe. Who are you, cruel one, greatest of gods? Be compassionate, for this is beyond me!'

'I am time, destroyer of the universe, grown ripe now and come to kill these men. Even if *you* don't fight, all these warriors will still be crushed. So stand up and conquer, win your kingdom, for long ago they all earned death and were slain, and now you are only the tool. Give up your trembling and prepare for war.'

But when Arjuna heard this he just kept his hands together and went on shaking, and cowered and stammered:

'It is right that the world should praise you, that monsters should scatter before you, that all the host of perfected ones should bow low. Why not? You are the Great Self, beyond Brahman, you are the lord of all lords, imperishable, beyond both being and non-being. I was rash to call you comrade, to say "Hey Krishna, hey Yadava, hey friend!" I pulled your leg a lot, both in private and in front of other people. Forgive me for that. There is no one like you. I bow before you. I prostrate my body. Bear with me, as a father with a son, or a friend with a friend, or maybe like a lover with one he loves. I have seen the unseeable, and I am glad of it, but it splinters my mind with fear. Take back your other shape—please!'

'It was a favour to you, Arjuna,' said the blessed one. 'I showed you my ultimate nature, something never seen before. Not through the Vedas or through sacrifices or through study or rites or grim asceticism can I be seen like that, champion of the Kurus. But don't be troubled because you have seen such a grim vision. Don't be afraid. Be glad. Look again. I am once more what I was.'

And he was human again, in a chariot, on a battlefield.

'That's a relief,' said Arjuna. 'I feel myself again too.'

'It wasn't easy to see something like that,' said Krishna. 'There are gods in heaven craving such a vision, but it is only bhakti—love and loyalty to me—that earns it, not the Vedas or sacrifices or harsh austerity. Work for me devotedly, burner of enemies, without attachment, without hatreds. Make me your goal.'

12 THE YOGA OF LOYALTY AND LOVE

Arjuna asked: 'There are yogis who practise this bhakti of yours, and there are others who go after the changeless state. Which are better?'

'Those manage better who have faith in me, but the people who seek the changeless state, they also find me, although they have to work harder at it. It is difficult for embodied folk to see the unseen, to think the unthinkable. It needs my help, and I lift up those who ask me to, who worship me and meditate on me with unswerving trust. I lift them right up out of the slough of samsara, the cycle of death and birth.

'Perhaps you can't manage such dedication. If not, practise the yoga of concentration. If you can't manage that, then offer all your acts to me; work for me. If you can't manage even that, then try to be unselfish.

'A yogi who rises beyond hate for others, is kindly and compassionate, has escaped from "I" and "mine", is the same in pleasure and in pain, unified in himself, loyal and devoted—he is dear to me. Someone that the world doesn't recoil from, and who doesn't recoil from the world, who is free from lurches of emotion—he is dear to me. Someone who has no vain ambitions, is pure and skilled and without anxiety, unselfish in what he does and loyal to me—he is dear to me. Someone who doesn't loathe or exult, doesn't grieve or crave, who has got beyond good and evil—he is dear to me. Someone who is the same to an enemy as to a friend, is the same whether respected or maligned, is the same in heat and cold, untouched by praise or blame, accepts what comes, has no special place called home, is circumspect in speech and steady in mind, all in loyalty to me—he is dear to me. And those who have faith, accepting these deathless guiding words—they are very dear to me indeed.'

13 PURUSHA AND PRAKRITI

'Krishna, what exactly is this nature of yours that we call Prakriti? And who is the person we call Purusha? And the field, what is it, and who is the one called the knower of the field? What is knowledge, and what is the thing to be known? Tell me these things, Krishna.'

'Your body is the field, son of Queen Pritha, and the atman is the knower. But in the world at large I am the knower of all the fields, and that knowledge is the ultimate knowledge. There are a lot of different doctrines about this, in hymns and sutras concerning the nature of brahman—and these sutras are well-argued and conclusive. All your likes and dislikes, pleasures and pains, intelligence and courage and the like—they happen in the field. Knowledge of course includes everything that I've been telling you here. It covers the shunning of conceit and deceit and the wish to do others harm; it covers the wish to be under control, detached and free from the ego, aware of what birth and death and old age and disease and pain really are. It is being detached, and not clinging on to sons and wives and property and the like—all that and bhakti, withdrawn from the jostling crowds, aware of the atman. That's knowledge—and everything else is ignorance.

'Brahman is the light beyond darkness, motionless yet moving, without beginning, surrounded by the eyes and ears and mouths and heads of the world, yet biding aloof from them all. It is both outside you and inside you, seated in your heart.

'But there is more to it than that, for the knower and the field are also Purusha and Prakriti. Prakriti is matter, and it is creator and creating and created all in one, while Purusha is her underlying cause, interwoven with her, experiencing her and caught up in her processes of birth. But again he isn't caught up at all, but watches, approves and experiences, quite apart. Anyone who knows these two—Purusha and Prakriti—and understands the binding strands called the gunas is not born again.

'There are some who come to realize this truth through meditation, but there are others who put their reason to work and infer it all. Still others discover it through what they do—and some indeed pick it up from them, and treasure it, and even these last can use it to overcome death. But appreciate this, Arjuna my stallion: Whatever exists, whether it moves or is still, is born out of the union of the knower and the field, a union of the nature that works and the nature that lies beyond work. As the sun lights up this world, so too does the lord of the field cast his light on all his domain.'

14 THE THREE GUNAS

'Nature is the womb in which I plant my seed, Arjuna, and from that act are born all these things that live and die in the circling ages. Whatever emerges from whatever womb, my nature is its mother and I am the seed-giving father.

'Prakriti has three strands, like a rope. These are the gunas that bind all the embodied selves, although such selves are changeless things. The gunas are called sattva, rajas and tamas. Sattva is pure and white, and gives health—its power to bind lies in the pull of happiness and learning. Rajas is passionate, welling up from red desire, and binds fast, son of Queen Pritha, in the grip of action. Tamas is born out of ignorance, a heavy dullness that leads all embodied folk astray into dark sloth, fecklessness and sleep. They are woven together, but in each man a particular strand will be the strongest.

'When the light of knowledge streams from all the body's gates, then sattva has increased. When greedy ambitious action springs up, then rajas has increased, my stallion. When negligence and delusion rule, then tamas has increased. When an embodied self comes face to face with death, sattva prevailing, it attains to a pure heaven; when death comes and rajas prevails, it is reborn among those who cling to actions; and when death comes and tamas prevails, it is born again in a deluded womb. The fruits of sattva are spotless, those of rajas are the pain that follows pleasure, while the fruits of tamas are ignorance. From sattva comes wisdom, from rajas greed, from tamas folly. Sattva leads upwards, while rajas leaves you in the midmost point, and tamas sends you down below. When an embodied self transcends them all, all these strands of existence, it is released from the wheel of birth and death and old age and pain, and wins to a deathless state.'

'How can we recognise such a man, lord?' asked Arjuna. 'How does he behave—how does he step beyond the three gunas?'

'He has no hatred for light or activity or delusion, nor does he pine in their absence. He sits indifferent, untouched by the strands. "They are busy at their work," he thinks, and stays firm-based and unshaken, looking on a clod of earth and a piece of gold as just the same, staying the same in good times as in bad, with friends as with enemies, seeking to perform no special acts, beyond the strands of nature. And with bhakti—loyalty and love for me—this servant rises into my changeless brahman.'

15 THE ETERNAL TREE

'There is an eternal fig tree,' said Krishna, 'with its roots up above and its branches down below. Its leaves are the Vedas, and if you appreciate this you understand the Vedas. Its branches extend all around, from earth to heaven, nourished by the gunas, and its twigs are the things you see and touch and hear and taste and smell. Its roots spread out below, twined in the doings of men. It is a puzzling tree, this fig with its well-nourished roots—its beginning and end and foundation are not understood here.

'Take up the axe of detachment, and cut that strange tree down! And then seek your freedom among those who are beyond illusion, beyond pleasure and pain, who dwell where the sun and the moon don't shine, because their light is not needed there. No one returns from that home.

'In the world of living things a tiny particle of me—no more than that—becomes a living self, wrapped around in nature's senses and the mind. When this free self takes on or leaves a body, it takes the sense-experiences with it, much as a wind might blow away the scent as it rises from its source. It enjoys the ear and the eye and touch and taste and smell, and enjoys the mind too. But whether the self is in or out of the body, in or out of the twining gunas, the ignorant do not see him—though with wisdom's eye he can be seen. Yogis see him in themselves, but others don't.

'I live in the sun and in the moon and in the earth and in plants—and also in every heart, creating memory and wisdom, dispelling doubts, writing the Vedas and the Vedanta. Here I have two natures, one passing and one permanent, but beyond them is a still higher form that sustains them both. The man who knows this, loyal to me and loving me, knows everything. That is the deepest teaching of them all, Arjuna, and all you need to know.'

16 THE DIVINE AND THE DEVILISH

'A good man has many qualities,' said Krishna. 'He is fearless and pure, steady and generous and restrained in his ways. He performs his sacrifices and studies the scriptures, lives in an austere way, hurting none, telling no lies, resisting anger, renouncing luxury, keeping the peace, avoiding insults, compassionate to all beings, not nagged by greed, but gentle, modest, consistent, ardent, patient, enduring, not treacherous or arrogant. A man like that is born to a god's destiny.

'A hypocrite is very different—vainglorious and arrogant in his ways, angry and harsh and boorish, born to a devil's destiny. A god's destiny means freedom, but a devil's destiny is enslavement.

'Don't worry, Arjuna! You were born to a god's destiny.

'There are two kinds of being in the world: the divine and the devilish. I have said rather a lot about the divine, so it is time to talk about the other kind. Devilish folk know nothing of the mysteries I have described. They say: "This world is chaotic and hasn't any law behind it, no god behind it, no ordered origin. Desire alone keeps it going." Believing this, these lost people do all sorts of destructive things. Their doings stem from greed. They are full of hypocrisy and vanity, burdened with frustration till the day they die, because they can't possibly fulfil all their desires. "I got this today," they announce, "and I've another whim to chase now. This wealth is mine, and soon I'll have more. He was my enemy and I killed him—and I'll kill more if need be. I'm master here, you know, and I'll take my pleasures where I will. What a strong happy successful fellow I am! I'm rich and well-born—who is my equal?

Now and again I sacrifice and maybe a bit of alms-giving here and there, but let's just have a good time!'' So they talk, these pathetic folk. Puffed up with their pride and offering empty sacrifices, they impel themselves to hell. I live in them as in everyone else, but they have no time for me, despising what I am. So birth follows death and death follows birth, in more and more devilish wombs, spiralling lower and lower. Desire, anger and greed are the three gates of hell, where they forget the self, the atman. They are gates worth escaping, Arjuna, so follow the dharma, and not your whims and fancies.'

17 KINDS OF FAITH

Arjuna asked: 'What happens to people who forsake our scriptures and do their worship elsewhere? What strand prevails in them?'

'Every man's faith is in accordance with his nature,' said the blessed one. 'Men with sattva prevailing in them sacrifice to the gods, but those with rajas prevailing sacrifice to demons, and those with tamas to ghosts and goblins. There are also those who forget scriptural law and—full of hyprocrisy and egotism, passion and desire—violently mortify their flesh, foolishly torturing the living elements of their body, and me too, deep inside them.

'We all love food, and there are three kinds of that too, each agreeing with the different kind of man. There are also three kinds of tapas, of austerity and penance; and there are three ways of sacrifice and worship, and three ways of giving alms.

'Sattvic foods lead to a fuller life, to strength and health and satisfaction. They are tasty, soft and oily, wholesome and gladdening to the heart. Rajasic foods, however, are pungent, sour, salty, sharp, stinging hot, rough and burning, and lead to pain, misery and sickness. And tamasic foods are stale and tasteless, rotten and decayed, leavings unfit for sacrifice.

'Sattvic sacrifice is the kind approved by scriptural law and offered up with no expectation of reward, but rather in a simple sense of duty. Rajasic sacrifice seeks rewards, and is done for show and nothing more than that, Arjuna best of heroes. And tamasic sacrifice is the kind that violates the law, where no food is distributed, no hymns are chanted and no fees are paid to brahmins.

'Due reverence to the gods and to the twice-born, to teachers and to wise men, along with purity, uprightness, continent study and non-violence—these are the true tapas of the body. Words that cause no harm, but are true and kind and pleasant, along with recitation of scriptures—these are the tapas of speech. Serenity of mind and kindliness, silence and self-control, and the purification of one's nature—these are the tapas of the mind. Men who have the highest faith, disciplined in their selves and unmindful of reward, they do tapas in this three-fold way, and tapas like that is sattvic. But there are others who mortify their bodies to win respect and honour and reverence, or simply for the sake of show, and tapas like that is rajasic, fickle and short-lived. And there is a tapas that is perverted, thriving on self-torture and aimed at injuring others. It is tamasic.

'Giving alms as a sacred duty, expecting no favours in return, at the proper time and place, to the right receivers, that is sattvic alms-giving. But alms given in the expectation of favours in return, or purely for the merit to be gained, and given when it hurts to give —that is rajasic. And alms given at the wrong time and in the wrong place to an unworthy receiver, without proper respect and in a contemptuous way—that is tamasic.

'Aum tat sat—Yes, that is how it is. This mantra is the three-fold pointer to brahman, the ancient source of the brahmins, the Vedas and the sacrifices. "Aum" initiates all acts of worship, all acts of giving, all acts of austerity. With "tat" all those who seek release perform their acts of worship, of alms-giving and of tapas, unmindful of rewards and with "sat" there is a sense of what is real and good, son of Pritha, in praiseworthy actions. But actions done without faith are "asat", valueless both in this world and in the next.'

18 SANNYASA

'Mighty-armed Krishna,' said Arjuna, 'I still need to be sure about sannyasa, about renunciation, and about the surrender of the self.'

'Sannyasa is just giving up actions that are snared in desire and pleasure,' said Krishna, 'and self-surrender is abandoning the fruits of effort. There are some who say that all actions must be given up, because they are all stained with vice. I assert that you can't give up worship and alms-giving and proper tapas, for they purify the wise — but they must be done with detachment. That is my final comment, son of Pritha. One can't renounce all action. To give up actions enjoined by scripture would be tamas, wouldn't it? To give up actions that are hard to do and cause one distress would be rajas, wouldn't it? But action performed simply because it *should* be performed, unmindful of its fruits—it is sattva. A self-surrendered man, filled with this sattva, wise and beyond doubt, doesn't recoil from disagreeable work or cling to what is congenial to him. No embodied self can give up all action, and so it is the *fruits* of action that must be surrendered.

'The fruits of one's actions are of three kinds too: the kind we want, the kind we don't want, and the mixed kind. If you haven't surrendered them they pile up after death. Someone who sees the inner atman as the doer of actions is unintelligent and perverse—but a man who has reached the ego-less state, his consciousness undefiled, even if he destroys a world, destroys nothing. He is unbound.

'The knowledge that sees everything as one and unchanging, undivided yet diverse—it is sattva. But the knowledge that sees all beings as disparate, different and distinct—that is rajas. And the knowledge that sticks to bits and pieces and never sees the whole at all, that narrow knowledge is tamas. A necessary act, performed with detachment, without love or hate, unmindful of reward—it is sattva. But an act that is strained, done by someone seeking his own ends and praising himself as he goes—it is rajas. And an act begun by a deluded man, taking no thought to the consequences or to loss or to injury or to his capacity for it—it is tamas. A person doing things, detached and steady, unchanged by failure or success, forgetting his ego—he is sattva. A person intent on reward, filled with passion, greedy, intent on doing harm, swayed up in exultation or plunging down in grief—he is rajas. A person doing things crassly, in a vulgar way, strutting about, cheating and speaking foully, slothful and depressed and taking too long about everything—he is tamas.

'The gunas rule.

'They rule too in the intellect, and in constancy of purpose. Buddhi, the intellect, if it can distinguish between action and its cessation, between what should and should not be, between danger and security, bondage and release—it is sattva. But if it can't see these clearly, it is rajas, and if it turns them right round, all things their opposite, it is tamas. The constancy of sattva is in restraining mind and breath and sense, unswerving in yoga, but the constancy of rajas is in clinging to pleasure, self-interest and justice, seeking reward. The constancy of tamas is in the fool who clings to sleep and fear and grief, to the swing of depression and elation.

'Pleasure is three-fold too. There is a pleasure that seems at first like poison, but later turns to ambrosia—it is sattva and found in the peace of understanding the self. There is also a pleasure that starts like ambrosia among the senses, but grows to be like poison—and that is rajas, passion's way. And there is a blind pleasure that leads astray from start to finish—it is tamas.

'No living creature on earth or in heaven is free from these three gunas that weave the rope of Prakriti, my nature.

'Consider the brahmins, the kshatriyas, the vaishyas and the shudras, Arjuna burner of enemies, each caste working according to the gunas, according to its nature. Brahmin priests are calm, restrained, ascetic, pure, long-suffering and upright, wise in both theory and practice, faithful, inheriting their nature. Kshatriya princes are heroic, ardent, enduring, skilful, steady in combat, generous and lordly, inheriting their nature. Vaishyas till the fields, protect the cattle and engage in trade, inheriting their nature—and the shudras perform tasks whose very essence is service. By doing the work proper to him, rejoicing in it, a man perfects himself; by dedicating it to the source of the activity of all beings, the spinner of the worlds, a man attains perfection. Better to do one's own duty, however badly, than to do someone else's, however well. There is no loss in doing the work for which one has been formed by nature, but in the work itself there can never be perfection, for all action is flaw-clouded, like fire with smoke—but it has still to be done, son of Pritha.

'The man whose consciousness is free, disciplined and without desire, he passes through sannyasa to perfection, transcending karma.

'All these things that I have urged upon you, he does them and does them well, becoming one with brahman, and through bhakti entering into me. Trust me, offer your actions to me, fix your mind on me, surrender to me, surmount all dangers through my grace—but if, through selfish egotism, you won't listen, then you will be lost. If you rely on your ego and think "I will not fight", then your resolve is empty. Nature will compel you. You are bound by your karma, son of Pritha, and what you deludedly think you won't do you *will* do, whether you like it or not!

'Arjuna, in the heart of all beings lives the lord, twirling them here and there by his potent maya. He alone is the refuge; seek him, with all your being and all your love, and so win peace. This is the highest mystery of all. You can pass these teachings on to those who care for me. That is a good thing to do, and brings you closer to me. But don't pass them on to frivolous folk, with no loyalty or love for me, the disobedient and the envious.

'Well then, Arjuna, you've listened. Has the confusion of your ignorance been swept away?'

'The confusion is destroyed,' said Arjuna, preparing himself. 'Your grace did it. I see things clearly now, and stand ready for the battle.'

Appendix
A Note on Translations and Versions of the Gita

The Bhagavad-Gita, as I have presented it here, is not a direct translation as such. Rather, it is a 'version', a somewhat simplified presentation from which various repetitious or obscure elements have been removed. It is also in fairly straightforward contemporary prose, where the original is Sanskrit verse and many modern renderings have been variously in archaic or biblical prose or verse.

By making it somewhat shorter and putting it in prose I have lost the convenience of chapter-and-verse reference and quotability, but have gained, I believe, in making the whole more accessible to modern readers. Because many of the more than fifty translations and versions of the *Gita* in the English language are rather difficult to get into, many people 'dip into' rather than 'read' their copies. We all of course have our preferences for styles in English: some prefer a more 'biblical' *Gita*, others look for something that is as close as possible to the spirit of the original Sanskrit. This *Gita* is intended to be a fairly easy read; it can be used in its own right, or as a springboard to more complex versions.

Every version of the *Gita* other than the Sanskrit original is, however, the *Gita* to some extent redrawn. What you have here is *The Bhagavad-Gita* through my eyes. You can also look at it through Annie Besant's eyes, or Sarvepalli Radhakrishnan's eyes, or Franklin Edgerton's, or Maharishi Mahesh Yogi's, or the eyes of Bhaktivedanta Swami Prabhupada of the Krishna Consciousness movement. These are all worth looking at, and in particular I would recommend the gentle Christian-mystical translation of Juan Mascaró (Penguin, 1962) as a general non-technical translation, and the magisterial *The Bhagavad-Gita* with detailed commentary by R.C. Zaehner (Oxford University Press, 1969). They all handle the material differently, and yet in the end the force of the original gets through each interpreter-into-English, to communicate something directly to the reader.

There are three main ways of rendering a work in one language into another: word-for-word crude translation that is hard to read but gives a powerful feeling of the original language; more-or-less literal translation that does however seek to be readable in the second language; and free translation, which seeks to embody the 'spirit' of the original text via the 'spirit' of the new language. All three styles have their strengths and their weaknesses, their defenders and their detractors. Let me demonstrate the various possibilities as regards the *Gita*.

To do this, I have taken verse 22 of Book 2, where the god Krishna describes to the hero Arjuna the nature of reincarnation. The cultural divide is best shown by first of all presenting the verse in the original devanagari script used for Sanskrit ('the divine urban script'), then presenting the Sanskrit in typical Roman transliteration:

(1) Verse 22, Book 2 in devanagari script:

वासांसि जीर्णानि यथा विहाय
नवानि गृह्णाति नरोऽपराणि ।
तथा शरीराणि विहाय जीर्णा-
न्यन्यानि संयाति नवानि देही ॥२२॥

(2) Verse 22, Book 2 in Roman transliteration:

vāsāṁsi jīrṇāni yathā vihāya
navāni gṛhṇāti naro 'parāṇi
tathā śarīrāṇi vihāya jīrṇāny
anyāni saṁyāti navāni dehī

Next, we can put the material through two stages of word-for-word literalism, the first where the English is 'bent' to resemble the original Sanskrit, the next where it is a close verse version of the original:

(3) word-for-word literalism:

clothes worn-out just-as casting-off
new-ones takes a-man others
in-the-same-way bodies casting-off worn-out
different-ones takes-on new the-embodied

(4) a close verse translation (Franklin Edgerton, *The Bhagavad-Gita,* Harvard University Press, 1944), where the Sanskrit *dehi*, 'the embodied' takes on an optional extra, 'the soul':

As leaving aside worn-out garments
A man takes other, new ones,
So leaving aside worn-out bodies
To other, new ones goes the embodied (soul).

Zaehner's translation demonstrates the next stage, as it were: a prose presentation that closely approximates to the original, and this time adds an optional 'self' rather than the loaded word 'soul' to the text:

(5) close approximation in prose:

As a man casts off his worn-out clothes and takes on other new ones, so does the embodied (self) cast off its worn-out bodies and enters other new ones.

Closer to normal English is the tight prose of Sarvepalli Radhakrishnan in *Indian Philosophy* (Princeton University Press, 1957, with Charles A. Moore); he holds true to the original while using 'soul' as an integral part of his text, not as an option:

(6) general approximation in prose:

Just as a person casts off worn-out garments and puts on others that are new, even so does the embodied soul cast off worn-out bodies and take on others that are new.

I would place Mascaró next. He makes what I see as a general adaptation of the original into prose, while keeping the verse order and numbers, making a variety of changes in grammar and vocabulary, such as plural instead of singular and the use of the masculine pronoun which, along with words like 'mortal' and 'Spirit', adds a Western, Christian and 'biblical' flavour to the whole:

(7) general adaptation (using biblical expressions and style)

As a man leaves an old garment and puts on one that is new, the Spirit leaves his mortal body and puts on one that is new.

Lastly comes my own, a prose style that condenses the original and does away with verse numbering, seeking to be non-Western and non-biblical in its approach but at the same time moving well away from the original densely packed Sanskrit style:

(8) free adaptation (somewhat colloquial, but seeking to avoid imposing Western cultural ideas on the text):

You know how easily a man changes his clothes; in the same way this inner something casts off its old worn body and takes on a new one.

There can be no perfect or ultimate 'true' version of the *Gita* (or the Bible, or the Quran, or any other exotic text) in English. Given various renderings, we all usually end up with our stylistic and presentational preferences, but at the same time it is possible to see different versions of the same original as having different uses on different occasions—and special values of their own. What Besant or Edgerton or Mascaró or McArthur or anyone else chose to do with a text like the *Gita* tells us something not only about the *Gita* but also about what it meant to those people and what it signified at the times when and the places where the work was done.

Index